Marriages, Deaths, Accidents,
Duels and Runaways
Compiled from

The Weekly Georgia Telegraph

Macon, Georgia
1854–1857

R. Newton Wilcox

Heritage Books
2009

HERITAGE BOOKS
AN IMPRINT OF HERITAGE BOOKS, INC.

Books, CDs, and more—Worldwide

For our listing of thousands of titles see our website at
www.HeritageBooks.com

Published 2009 by
HERITAGE BOOKS, INC.
Publishing Division
100 Railroad Ave. #104
Westminster, Maryland 21157

Copyright © 2002 R. Newton Wilcox

Other books by the author:

*Marriages, Deaths, Accidents, Duels and Runaways, Etc., Compiled from
The Weekly Georgia Telegraph, Macon, Georgia, 1826–1828*

*Marriages, Deaths, Accidents, Duels and Runaways, Etc., Compiled from
The Weekly Georgia Telegraph, Macon, Georgia, 1850–1853*

*Marriages, Deaths, Accidents, Duels and Runaways, Etc., Compiled from
The Weekly Georgia Telegraph, Macon, Georgia, 1854–1857*

*Marriages, Deaths, Accidents, Duels and Runaways, Etc., Compiled from
The Weekly Georgia Telegraph, Macon, Georgia, 1858–1860*

All rights reserved. No part of this book may be reproduced or transmitted in any form or by any means, electronic or mechanical, including photocopying, recording or by any information storage and retrieval system without written permission from the author, except for the inclusion of brief quotations in a review.

International Standard Book Numbers
Paperbound: 978-0-7884-2248-5
Clothbound: 978-0-7884-8228-1

TABLE OF CONTENTS

ISSUE OF JANUARY 3, 1854	11
ISSUE OF JANUARY 10, 1854	11
ISSUE OF JANUARY 17, 1854	14
ISSUE OF JANUARY 24, 1854	15
ISSUE OF JANUARY 31, 1854	16
ISSUE OF FEBRUARY 7, 1854	17
ISSUE OF FEBRUARY 14, 1854	19
ISSUE OF FEBRUARY 21, 1854	21
ISSUE OF FEBRUARY 28, 1854	23
ISSUE OF MARCH 7, 1854	25
ISSUE OF MARCH 14, 1854	26
ISSUE OF MARCH 28, 1854	27
ISSUE OF APRIL 4, 1854	28
ISSUE OF APRIL 18, 1854	30
ISSUE OF APRIL 25, 1854	30
ISSUE OF MAY 2, 1854	31
ISSUE OF MAY 16, 1854	32
ISSUE OF MAY 23, 1854	32
ISSUE OF MAY 30, 1854	34
ISSUE OF JUNE 6, 1854	35
ISSUE OF JUNE 13, 1854	35
ISSUE OF JUNE 20, 1854	36
ISSUE OF JULY 18, 1854	37
ISSUE OF JULY 25, 1854	38
ISSUE OF AUGUST 1, 1854	39

ISSUE OF AUGUST 8, 1854	39
ISSUE OF AUGUST 22, 1854	40
ISSUE OF AUGUST 29, 1854	41
ISSUE OF SEPTEMBER 5, 1854	42
ISSUE OF SEPTEMBER 12, 1854	43
ISSUE OF SEPTEMBER 19, 1854	44
ISSUE OF SEPTEMBER 26, 1854	46
ISSUE OF OCTOBER 3, 1854	48
ISSUE OF OCTOBER 10, 1854	49
ISSUE OF OCTOBER 17, 1854	50
ISSUE OF OCTOBER 24, 1854	52
ISSUE OF OCTOBER 31, 1854	52
ISSUE OF NOVEMBER 7, 1854	53
ISSUE OF NOVEMBER 14, 1854	54
ISSUE OF NOVEMBER 21, 1854	54
ISSUE OF NOVEMBER 28, 1854	55
ISSUE OF DECEMBER 5, 1854	56
ISSUE OF DECEMBER 12, 1854	57
ISSUE OF DECEMBER 19, 1854	58
ISSUE OF DECEMBER 26, 1854	58
ISSUE OF JANUARY 2, 1855	59
ISSUE OF JANUARY 9, 1855	61
ISSUE OF JANUARY 16, 1855	61
ISSUE OF JANUARY 23, 1855	62
ISSUE OF JANUARY 30, 1855	63
ISSUE OF FEBRUARY 6, 1855	65

ISSUE OF FEBRUARY 13, 1855 66
ISSUE OF FEBRUARY 20, 1855 66
ISSUE OF FEBRUARY 27, 1855 67
ISSUE OF MARCH 6, 1855 68
ISSUE OF MARCH 13, 1855 68
ISSUE OF MARCH 27, 1855 69
ISSUE OF APRIL 10, 1855 69
ISSUE OF APRIL 17, 1855 70
ISSUE OF APRIL 24, 1855 71
ISSUE OF MAY 1, 1855 71
ISSUE OF MAY 8, 1855 72
ISSUE OF MAY 29, 1855 73
ISSUE OF JUNE 12, 1855 74
ISSUE OF JUNE 19, 1855 75
ISSUE OF JUNE 26, 1855 75
ISSUE OF JULY 3, 1855 76
ISSUE OF JULY 10, 1855 77
ISSUE OF JULY 17, 1855 77
ISSUE OF JULY 24, 1855 78
ISSUE OF JULY31, 1855 78
ISSUE OF AUGUST 7, 1855 79
ISSUE OF AUGUST 14, 1855 80
ISSUE OF AUGUST 21, 1855 82
ISSUE OF AUGUST 28, 1855 83
ISSUE OF SEPTEMBER 4, 1855 83
ISSUE OF SEPTEMBER 11, 1855 83

ISSUE OF SEPTEMBER 18, 1855 83
ISSUE OF SEPTEMBER 25, 1855 84
ISSUE OF OCTOBER 1, 1855 84
ISSUE OF OCTOBER 23, 1855 87
ISSUE OF OCTOBER 30, 1855 88
ISSUE OF NOVEMBER 6, 1855 90
ISSUE OF NOVEMBER 13, 1855 92
ISSUE OF NOVEMBER 20, 1855 92
ISSUE OF NOVEMBER 27, 1855 93
ISSUE OF DECEMBER 4, 1855 93
ISSUE OF DECEMBER 11, 1855 95
ISSUE OF DECEMBER 18, 1855 95
ISSUE OF DECEMBER 25, 1855 96
ISSUE OF JANUARY 1, 1856 97
ISSUE OF JANUARY 8, 1856 98
ISSUE OF JANUARY 15, 1856 98
ISSUE OF JANUARY 22, 1856 98
ISSUE OF JANUARY 29, 1856 101
ISSUE OF FEBRUARY 5, 1856 103
ISSUE OF FEBRUARY 12, 1856 103
ISSUE OF FEBRUARY 19, 1856 104
ISSUE OF FEBRUARY 26, 1856 105
ISSUE OF MARCH 4, 1856 106
ISSUE OF MARCH 11, 1856 107
ISSUE OF MARCH 18, 1856 108
ISSUE OF MARCH 25, 1856 109

ISSUE OF APRIL 8, 1856 110
ISSUE OF APRIL 15, 1856 111
ISSUE OF APRIL 22, 1856 112
ISSUE OF APRIL 29, 1856 113
ISSUE OF MAY 6, 1856 114
ISSUE OF MAY 13, 1856 115
ISSUE OF MAY 27, 1856 115
ISSUE OF JUNE 3, 1856 116
ISSUE OF JUNE 10, 1856 118
ISSUE OF JUNE 17, 1856 119
ISSUE OF JUNE 24, 1856 119
ISSUE OF JULY 1, 1856 120
ISSUE OF JULY 8, 1856 121
ISSUE OF JULY15, 1856 122
ISSUE OF JULY 22, 1856 123
ISSUE OF JULY 29, 1856 124
ISSUE OF AUGUST 5, 1856 125
ISSUE OF AUGUST 12, 1856 125
ISSUE OF AUGUST 19, 1856 126
ISSUE OF AUGUST 26, 1856 127
ISSUE OF SEPTEMBER 2, 1856 127
ISSUE OF SEPTEMBER 9, 1856 128
ISSUE OF SEPTEMBER 23, 1856 129
ISSUE OF OCTOBER 7, 1856 129
ISSUE OF OCTOBER 21, 1856 130
ISSUE OF OCTOBER 28, 1856 131

ISSUE OF NOVEMBER 4, 1856 132
ISSUE OF NOVEMBER 18, 1856 132
ISSUE OF NOVEMBER 25, 1856 133
ISSUE OF DECEMBER 2, 1856 133
ISSUE OF DECEMBER 16, 1856 133
ISSUE OF DECEMBER 23, 1856 134
ISSUE OF DECEMBER 30, 1856 134
ISSUE OF JANUARY 6, 1857 135
ISSUE OF JANUARY 13, 1857 135
ISSUE OF JANUARY 20, 1857 137
ISSUE OF JANUARY 27, 1857 138
ISSUE OF FEBRUARY 3, 1857 138
ISSUE OF FEBRUARY 10, 1857 139
ISSUE OF FEBRUARY 17, 1857 139
ISSUE OF MARCH 3, 1857 141
ISSUE OF MARCH 17, 1857 142
ISSUE OF MARCH 31, 1857 142
ISSUE OF APRIL 7, 1857 142
ISSUE OF APRIL 14, 1857 143
ISSUE OF APRIL 21, 1857 143
ISSUE OF APRIL 28, 1857 143
ISSUE OF MAY 5, 1857 144
ISSUE OF MAY 12, 1857 145
ISSUE OF MAY 19, 1857 145
ISSUE OF MAY 26, 1857 146
ISSUE OF JUNE 2, 1857 147

ISSUE OF JUNE 9, 1857 147

ISSUE OF JUNE 23, 1857 147

ISSUE OF JUNE 30, 1857 148

ISSUE OF JULY 7, 1857 149

ISSUE OF JULY 14, 1857 149

ISSUE OF JULY 21, 1857 151

ISSUE OF JULY 28, 1857 152

ISSUE OF AUGUST 11, 1857 152

ISSUE OF AUGUST 18, 1857 153

ISSUE OF SEPTEMBER 1, 1857 153

ISSUE OF SEPTEMBER 8, 1857 153

ISSUE OF SEPTEMBER 15, 1857 154

ISSUE OF SEPTEMBER 22, 1857 156

ISSUE OF SEPTEMBER 29, 1857 156

ISSUE OF OCTOBER 5, 1857 156

ISSUE OF OCTOBER 13, 1857 156

ISSUE OF OCTOBER 20, 1857 157

ISSUE OF NOVEMBER 10, 1857 158

ISSUE OF NOVEMBER 17, 1857 158

ISSUE OF DECEMBER 8, 1857 159

ISSUE OF DECEMBER 15, 1857 160

ISSUE OF DECEMBER 22, 1857 160

Issue of January 3, 1854

Funeral of MR. CAMPBELL – Both houses of Congress, the President, cabinet, and Foreign Ministers, attended the funeral of the Hon. BROOKINS CAMPBELL of Tennessee, on Wednesday, at Washington.

Married – On the 20th December, by JAMES G. BARNES, Esq. MR. S. J. MCMILLON, formerly of Jackson, to Miss MARY V. COX, of Putnam.

On the 27th, in Crawford county, MR. B G. LOCKETT to Miss SALLIE R. BRIDGES of Culloden.

Died – In this city, on the 1st instant, EDWIN B. WEED, aged 47 years.

Issue of January 10, 1854

Attempt to Escape – We learn from the Milledgeville Recorder that on Tuesday night last, a bold attempt was made by several of the convicts in the Georgia Penitentiary to effect their escape. The ring leaders were JOHN SMITH and WELLS of Morgan county, the notorious DR. ROBERTS. SMITH succeeded in getting out of the cell building; the others, some four or five in number, only succeeded in getting out their cells into the passage. It was fortunate, remarks the Recorder, that the plot was discovered in time, as it is believed quite a number were concerned in this daring attempt to break prison, though the cells of only four of the prisoners were found unlocked. There are now 149 convicts in the Penitentiary, and the utmost vigilance should be exercised...

Death of MR. E. B. WEED – On Sunday, the 11th instant, MR. E. B. WEED, one of our oldest merchants and most respected citizens, expired at his residence in Macon after a very protracted and painful illness. Afflicted for many years with a pulmonary disease, death came upon him not unexpectedly...

Died in this city, on the morning of the 8th inst., Col. O. H. THROOP, in the 47th year of his age. Col. THROOP was a native of New York, but has resided in Macon for the last three years.

A man named HENDERSON was killed in Hancock county, Ga. on Saturday the 2_th ult., by a man named MCREA, during a drunken frolic.

An Affecting Scene – A few days ago, as DANIEL CULLEN was about to be taken from the jail, in St. Louis, to the State Penitentiary, to which he had been sentenced 99 years for the murder of his wife, an affecting scene occurred, which is thus related.
"Shortly before the arrival of the coach, a woman, bowed and decrepid with years, and bearing an infant in her arms, entered the office, hesitatingly. Scanning the faces of the crowd, her eye fell finally upon CULLEN and with a shriek of recognition, pain, and half joy, it appeared, she ran to him and fell weeping on his breast. It was his mother, come to bid him farewell, and show him his own child, for the last time. The scene was a moving one. The man, at first, was ashamed to give way to his feelings, and for awhile remonstrated greatly with his old mother as she fondled with him. At last, however, nature could contain itself no longer – he fell back upon his seat and cried like a child. The marshal and jailer, with all their familiarity with distress of the kind, found difficulty _____ their own promptings.

Recapture of an Escaped Bank Robber – In November, 1852, JOHN RAND was tried at Norfolk for robbing the Farmer's Branch Bank, Portsmouth, Va., of about $60,000, and was convicted and sentenced to ten years in the State Prison, but while in jail at Norfolk, awaiting a decision on exceptions which had been filed, he managed to effect his escape. This was a year ago. Officers from Virginia arrived in this city last week in search of RAND, who was not to be found, and they returned home leaving authority with Constable CLAPP for his arrest. Yesterday, RAND was seen in Court St. by Constable HOPKINS, who immediately notified Constable CLAPP, and he was shortly again in custody. In default of $60,000 bail he was committed to jail to await a requisition from the Governor of Virginia – RAND effected his escape in this way: Two females from Boston arrived at Norfolk, and, as is the custom there, were allowed unrestricted intercourse with the prisoner. One night the females gave an entertainment in the jail, at which the jailor and RAND were present. During the entertainment the females managed to obtain the jailor's key, and they and RAND walked off together. Boston Traveler, 27th

A Robber Caught – We learn from Y. J. ANDERSON, Esq, of Laurens county, that MR. HARDY SMITH who resides ten miles south of Dublin, was robbed of $2,400, in notes and bank bills, on the night of the 3d inst., under the following circumstances. On the evening of the 1st inst., a man who gave his name as JOSEPH WILSON called at Smith's home and asked for lodgings. He was received, and during the evening called for pen and paper, to remit some money to a person by the name of JOHN P. HALL of Savannah. He pretended to enclose $20 in small bills, and then called Smith's attention to the bulky appearance of the letter. SMITH very naturally proffered him a $20 bill, in exchange. In this way it is supposed that WILSON discovered where he kept his money. On the night of the 3d, Smith's house was entered, and the money and notes abstracted. The circumstances fixed suspicion at once upon WILSON. Messengers were dispatched in all directions, and the police of the several towns, placed on the alert. On the night of the 5th inst., MR. IVERN of Washington county, discovered that WILSON had taken lodgings at a house in his neighborhood. Having collected some friends, he repaired to the house. WILSON discovered their approach, and made his escape. After pursuing him for half a mile, he was overtaken by dogs, and captured; not, however, until he had drawn his boots under pretense of keeping off his assailants. His object in doing this was doubtless to throw away the money, as none was found upon his person. He has been lodged in the jail at Dublin, for trial at the next term of the Superior Court.

Married – On Thursday evening the 6th instant, by the Rev. S. LANDRUM, Col. WILLIAM G. HARRIS, to MISS ELIZA A. E. daughter of the Hon. JOHN BAILY, all of Bibb county, Ga.

Died – At his residence in Houston county, on the morning of the 27th inst., MR. ZACHARIAH LAMAR, of Pneumonia, after a distressing illness of seventeen days. MR. LAMAR was in his forty-sixth year, and has been a resident of this county for fourteen or fifteen years...He has left a wife and six children...

Issue of January 17, 1854

Homicide in Milledgeville – On the 11th instant, WM. A. RALSTON, a resident of this place, was killed in Milledgeville by ARCHIBALD HUNT, of Albany. RALSTON was standing in from of McCombs Hotel, conversing with a gentleman, when HUNT approached him, familiarly saying, "Well, DICK, you got me" – alluding, it is said, to a gaming transaction which had previously occurred between them. RALSTON enquired what he meant, but HUNT merely repeated the words. RALSTON then enquired if he meant to charge him with cheating, to which, we understand, HUNT replied, "yes, I do". At which RALSTON gave him the lie, and threw back a cloak which he was wearing. Hunt immediately drew a pistol and shot him through the heart, and RALSTON fell exclaiming "he has killed me". HUNT made some attempt to escape, but was soon captured and is now in the hands of the proper authorities, awaiting his trial. It is said that there had been some previous difficulty, but the parties had afterwards seem to be reconciled. RALSTON had no weapons of any kind about his person – not even a penknife.

Married – In Knoxville, on the 25th ult., MISS SARAH R. BRIDGES of Culloden, to MR. BENJAMIN LOCKETT of Hopewell.

On Wednesday evening, 11th instant, by Rev. JOHN MARSHAL, MR. C W. NIXON of Marshalville, Ga., and MISS MARY Y., youngest daughter of SOLOMON FUDGE, Esq. of Houston co., Ga.

Died – In this city, on the 5th inst., MR. JOHN W. TUCKER, aged about 31 years and 4 months.

At the Georgia Academy for the Blind, after a brief illness, of pneumonia, ANDREW J. ADDISON, in his 19th year. The deceased was a native of Habersham county, Ga., from early infancy he had suffered the loss of sight...

On the 5th instant, near Thomaston, MRS. JANE COBB, wife of Maj. WM. A. COBB. MRS. C. had been for many years a member of the Methodist Church, and died as she had lived, a Christian.

Issue of January 24, 1854

A Duel – A duel was fought near Memphis in Pickens county, Ala., on Saturday morning last, by Dr. F. W. IRBY and DR. FANT, of Norub___ county, in this state, in which the former was killed at the first fire, the ball entering his breast below the right nipple, passing through his heart and body. His remains were interred in the Odd Fellows' burying ground in this city on Monday.

The weapons were dueling pistols and the distance 13 ½ paces. DR. IRBY, who was killed, was a most estimable gentleman, a member elect of the present Legislature, and the difficulty grew out of some misunderstanding in the late canvass between himself and the antagonist, who was a candidate for the same station. Both gentlemen were Democrats and members of the Church – We are told that the affair would have taken place long since, had it not been for the extreme ill health of DR. IRBY, who was conveyed to the ground of combat in a carriage, and was scarcely able to stand up without support at the time of the fatal occurrence – the like of which we hope never again to be under the necessity of chronicling.   Columbus, Miss. Argus

Issue of January 31, 1854

Railroad Accident on the Charleston and Augusta Road – The mail train from Augusta when near LONRY's Turn Out, ran off the track this morning. Three cars were smashed. The Rev. MR. BAIRD, Editor of the Southern Presbyterian, was badly injured, also a brake-man. The cars arrived here this evening at half-past six o'clock.

Death of CAPT. PARTRIDGE – We learn by letter from Norwich, Vermont that Captain ALDEN PARTRIDGE, well known as the capable and intelligent head of several military academies, died at that place on the morning of Tuesday, the 17th instant. He was taken ill on Saturday evening, and his disease made rapid progress to its fatal termination. He was an excellent citizen, devoted to military education, and much beloved by his relatives and a wide circle of acquaintances. He was principal of the Military Institute at Brandywine Springs, the buildings of which were destroyed by fire a few weeks ago.   Pha. Bulletin

MR. O'DONOHOE, the Irish exile, died at Brooklyn, N. Y., on Sunday, in a very destitute condition.

Funeral of M. DE BODISCO – The funeral of M. DE BODISCO was largely attended at Georgetown, D. C. on Wednesday. The President, Heads of Departments, and the Foreign Ministers, were among the number present.

WALTER B. TOWNSEND, Esq. an eminent merchant of New York, was accidently killed in the city on Tuesday night.

Died – At Newark, N. J., on the morning of the 24th, CORNELIA J. TAYLOR, wife of A. A. ROFF and daughter of CHARLES TAYLOR, Esq.

The Drowned Officers of the San Francisco – Major and Brevet Lieutenant Colonel JOHN MARSHALL WASHINGTON, of the United States Army, who was swept from the deck of the San Francisco soon after her troubles commenced, was one of the most useful, as he had made himself one of the most distinguished artillery officers belonging to the service...

Issue of February 7, 1854

Death of MR. RICKER – We regret to announce the sudden death of MR. EDWARD F. RICKER, late superintendent of the Muscogee Railroad. He died at Perrysburg, S. C. on Monday of pneumonia. MR. RICKER was a native of this city, but for several years past has resided at Columbus, where he superintended the Muscogee Railroad. He came to this city about ten days since, and at the time of his death was on a visit to his wife's relations. His remains were brought to Savannah yesterday afternoon, and will be consigned to the grave this morning at 10 o'clock by the Republican Blues, of which corps he was for a number of years an active member. He leaves behind him a wife, a mother and many friends to mourn his early and sudden death. Savannah News, 1st Instant

We learn that a difficulty a few miles from West Point, Georgia, on Thursday morning of last week, between a young man named ROBT. HOUGH and another named CALEB WALKER, in which the latter had his skull broken with an axe by the former, from which he died that evening.

Killed By The Cars – A little boy named ANSLEY, ten or eleven years old, says the Atlanta Intelligencer, was run over by the cars on the Georgia railroad, in that city on Wednesday evening. He was attempting to jump on one of the cars from a platform, when missing his hold, he fell across the track, and three cars passed over his body, killing him instantly.

Died – At Tarversville, Twiggs county, of Congestive Fever, on the 24th of September 1853, MADISON ABERNATHY, son of SIGNAL RAINEY, in the 4th year of his age.

At the same place, of Inflammation of the Brain, on the 11th of January 1854, JAMES SIGNAL, son of SIGNAL RAINEY, in the 19th year of his age.

At the same place, of Typhus Fever, on the 16th of January 1854, SIGNAL RAINEY, in the 53d year of his age. MR. RAINEY was an acceptable member of the Baptist Church, an honest, intelligent and good citizen. He has left a disconsolate wife and four children to realize the bitterness of widowhood and orphanage.

$50 Reward – Runaway from the subscriber on the 19th of November last, in Pulaski county, Ga., about 11 miles from Hawkinsville, a negro woman named ANN. She is black, with small teeth, one out in front, balance sound; when spoken to, she throws her head back and answers quick. She is about 28 years old, and about five feet six or eight inches high, no other mark recollected.

The above reward of fifty dollars will be paid for her delivery to any safe jail.

M. R. SHARP

$200 Reward – Runaway from the subscriber, about the 1st of May 1850, his negro man JARRATT, at that time hired to MR. GREGORY in Macon, Ga. The said negro is about 26 or 27 years old, about 5 feet 11 inches high, rather spare made, dark copper color. He is supposed to be lurking either in Bladen or Sampson counties. The above reward will be paid for the delivery of said negro to me, or his lodgement in any jail, so I can get him again.

D. MCDANIEL
Wilmington, N. C.

Unexpected Return – The aeronaut, M. ARBAN, who made an ascent from Barcelona, Spain more than two years ago, and had not since been heard of, and who was believed to have fallen into the sea, and been drowned, has made his appearance again. An allicant letter says that his balloon went over to Africa, and that he was seized and made a slave, and continued in that state for two years, when he made his escape.

<u>Issue of February 14, 1854</u>

Brutal Murder – We learn says the Savannah Courier, that an affray took place on the Plank Road (West Broad Street) on Saturday night, in which a young man named BLUNT, was so badly beaten that he died yesterday morning. There is so far nothing, save a cap and jacket, left on the ground where the affray occurred to guide to the perpetrators of this foul deed. The young man BLUNT, we learn, was unassuming and industrious. The verdict of the Coroner's Jury is, that the deceased came to his death from blows inflicted by hands unknown.

Railroad Casualties – On Wednesday last a portion of a burthen train on the Susquehanna railroad broke loose whilst going up the summit, and ran back against an engine. Seven burthen cars were broken up, and one took fire and burnt up. A brakeman had both his feet badly crushed.
 On Tuesday last the wife of MR. JOHN ANGHE, residing near Hanover, Pa., was run over and horribly mangled by a railroad train. She was dead when taken up. It is supposed she threw herself under the train, while afflicted by insanity.

Highway Robbery – On Thursday night last, as MR. MEYER was returning to the city, when opposite the farm of MR. ISAAC HENRY, on the Washington road, he was accosted by a man, who asked him for a chew of tobacco. He had no sooner done so, than another man, (both disguised) stepped up and demanded his money. MR. MEYER, succeeded in breaking loose from the robbers, but he had not proceeded far, when one of them drew a pistol and shot him in the leg, bringing him to the ground. They then stripped him of every thing valuable they could find about him, including over one hundred dollars in money and left him in the road. By repeated and _____ cries, assistance reached him, but the robbers could not be traced. His friends have offered a reward of twenty-five dollars for the apprehension of these robbers, and it will be seen by the mayor's proclamation, that the city authorities offer a further reward of one hundred dollars for their arrest, with proof to _____. Augusta Constitutionalist

$20 Reward – Ranaway from the subscriber, on the night of the first of this month, two negroes, KEZZIAH, a woman about twenty-five years old, of a bright complexion, tolerably thick made, speaks quick when spoken to, and FANNY, a girl about seventeen years old, very slender made, of a yellow complexion, and a little stoop shouldered. I will pay the above reward for the delivery of them to me at my residence near Macon, Twiggs Co., Ga., or in any safe jail so that I can get them.

SIMON N. BECKCOM

Issue of February 21, 1854

A very sudden death occurred in Albany, Ga. on the 11th inst. A young man named DAVIS was found dead by his companions in the camp where they had passed the night. He made no noise or movement sufficient to awake any one during the night and apparently had died without a struggle. No inquest was held on the body, but a committee of Physicians after an examination held, gave it as their opinion that over exercise the day before, and the subsequent exposure brought on a malignant chill which caused his death. What rendered this opinion more probable was the fact that he had recently had an attack of chill and fever. The young man was moving from Marion to Thomas county.

A Centenarian – DANIEL JOHNSON, a revolutionary hero, aged 102 years, died in Copish county, Miss., on the 10th ult. He was a native of South Carolina, and served under Gen. MARION, and afterwards fought under Captain BARBER, in Georgia. He was also in the Creek War.

JOHN LITTLE, the assistant steward of the steamship Arabia, has been arrested in Boston on the charge of smuggling.

Heavy damages for personal injuries are becoming quite frequent. The administration of MR. MCCLOSKEY, who was killed by a collision on the Pennsylvania Railroad last March, have obtained a verdict of $4,500 against the company in one of the Pittsburgh courts, and at New Orleans a MR. GOULD has recovered $10,000 damages against the firm of Gardiner, Loger & Co. for false imprisonment.

A Dreadful Occurrence – About a week since the dwelling of MR. JAMES HARVEY, of Bullock county, was consumed by fire, together with his wife and infant, only three weeks old. MR. H. had gone out to work in one of his fields after breakfast, leaving his wife and child in bed, and after he had been gone for some time, looking in the direction of his house he saw it enveloped in flames. Hurrying to the rescue of his little family, he discovered neither sign nor sound of them. A few charred bones of the wife were the only sad evidence of the melancholy fate of herself and child. It is supposed that after MR. H. left the house, a log or stick rolled from the fire to the floor, thus setting fire to the house, and that MRS. H., being asleep became suffocated with the smoke and was thus unable to escape her dreadful death.

Savannah News

Two men calling themselves JOHN MORAN and JOHN FORD alias DIVINE charged with the murder of JOHN S. BLOUNT, an account of which was published in the News of the 7th inst., were arrested on board the State of Georgia, on her late arrival at Philadelphia, by officers WOOD and MERRELL of that city; Captain E. M. PRENDERGAST, of this city, having instructed them by telegraph to make the arrest. Through the indefatigable exertion of officer PRENDERGAST and WARING RUSSELL (the latter of whom bids fair to rival the character of the celebrated JACK HAYS in his profession) to ferret out the perpetrators of this terrible deed, sufficient evidence was produced before the Grand Jury to warrant that body in finding a true bill against the accused and justify their arrest.   Sav. News

Reward – The Governor of the State offers a reward of $350 for the apprehension and delivery of JOHN MORAN and JOHN FORD, alias DIVINE, charged with the murder of JNO. BLOUNT who, our readers will remember, was brutally assailed not long since, and has since died of his wounds. The Proclamation also offers a reward of $150 for either of the two fugitives should they be taken separately. The following is the description of their persons.
JOHN MORAN is about 5 feet 7 inches high, weighs from 150 to 160, complexion light, florid, light sandy hair, and stoops a little in the shoulders, an Irishman by birth.
JOHN FORD alias DIVINE, height about 6 feet, weighs about 160 to 175, complexion fair, sharp visage, blue eyes, sandy hair, walks straight, and when speaking has a down cast look, an Irishman by birth.

Issue of February 28, 1854

Gen. ARMSTRONG, editor and proprietor of the Washington Union, died on Friday, at Washington, of congestion of the brain.

It is stated here, on high authority, the MR. FILLMORE is about to lead to the altar MISS ELIZABETH PORTER, of Niagara Falls, only daughter of the late Gen. PETER B. PORTER, a hero of the War of 1812, and Secretary of War under JOHN QUINCY ADAMS. MISS PORTER is 32 years of age, and a lady of superior intellect, high cultivation, and large fortune. Her brother and herself are the sole heirs of their father's great estate, including Goat Island and other lucrative property as Niagara Falls. MISS PORTER has long been a reigning belle in Western New York, and has refused many an eligible parti, it is said.

"The Woman Soldier" – We have already mentioned that a petition was before Congress from MRS. ELIZABETH G. SMITH of Missouri, for pay and bounty land, in reward for service rendered during the Mexican War. She performed a soldier's duty for 10 months, before her sex was discovered, and was known in her company by the name of "BILL NEWCOMB". The Senate has awarded her 10 months wages, three months extra pay, and 160 acres of land.

The Arrest of Madame RESTELL – The _____ of Madame RESTELL, in New York, bids ____ to be a very serious one. The complainant is a young woman named CORDELIA A. GRANT, aged 22, who has made affidavit that she has lived for seven years with GEO. R. SHACKFORD, of Fordham, Westchester county, N. Y. who has repeatedly promised to marry her, but never done so; that during this time she has been five times enciente, and each time Madame RESTELL was employed by SHACKFORD to destroy her child. The details are, many of them, unfit for the press, but the criminality of Madame RESTELL, her reputed husband, LOHMAN, and SHACKFORD, the seducer, is directly alleged. The young woman is from Portland, Me. SHACKFORD has lately built an elegant house at Fordham.

An Aged Miser – A man named HEAVING, died at Chilcompton, Somersetshire, aged 98. He denied himself of almost every necessary, either food, fire or clothing. A fortnight since he was visited by a lady, who gave him a shilling, as he told her he was perishing from cold and want of food. He had the tale for anyone who went to see him. After his death there was discovered his about the cottage nearly 2000 lbs., principally in guineas and half guineas, several suits of clothes, rotten from lying by, and a quantity of coal bought by him twenty-one years since, and which he was too niggardly to burn. There was also found a will, wherein he bequeathed 300 lbs., which it seems he had put out at interest, with his other money etc. to some relatives in America, leaving a poor old relative, who had rendered him every assistance in her power, without a shilling.   English paper

Issue of March 7, 1854

Mail Rider Turned Robber and Decamped – A late number of the Camden Republic chronicled the disappearance of J. D. GUNN, mail rider between that place and Catawba, under suspicious circumstances. He was seen at Rehoboth on the 3d ult. and on the Monday following a package of letters, broken open, was found partly buried at the foot of a fallen tree. On examination, it was found that these letters were mostly mailed at Camden, and a trap was set to catch the rider of his return, but he was too smart for the trappers, and sent the mail back by another person, who reported him on an excursion to Georgia. Since the publication of the Republic, MR. C M. COCHRAN, postmaster of Cambridge, located on this route, states in a letter to the Dallas Gazette, that on the day mentioned, the said GUNN robbed the Cambridge mails, and intimates pretty clearly that GUNN had gone off, if not half-cocked, at least prematurely...

Swindlers in Augusta – The Chronicle, of the 25th, says two young men of genteel appearance, very well dressed, who registered their names at the hotel as JOHN B. HOLLINSMAN and HENRY A. DUFEY, were arrested in that city a few days since on a charge of swindling. On examination before Justice OLIN, they were committed for trial on three charges of swindling, and one for an attempt to swindle. It appears that one of them would loiter around some secluded part of the city, while the other would meet his accomplice, who would propose a bet, the accomplice would take the bet, and borrow all the victim's money by pledging a worthless check, drawn on some bank in the city, by some fictitious firm, and promise to return to the hotel immediately, and redeem the check by replacing the money. In this way the rogues have succeeded in obtaining several hundred dollars. They are to have further examination on another charge.

On Thursday morning last, JACOB L. ABRAMS, one of the first citizens of Coweta county, Ga. was found dead in his house a few miles from Newnan. He lived secluded from house and family, and denied himself all the comforts of life, though possessed of an estate valued at $20,000.

An incident occurred at Augusta on Monday afternoon which was nearly a melancholy catastrophe. As a number of ladies were standing on the Railroad Bridge over the Canal, viewing the progress of the flood, an engine approached which frightened them from their position. One lady was so alarmed that she jumped over the railing into the water, which was at that point ten or twelve feet deep, and must have drowned had she not been speedily rescued. MR. JOHN GOWDY gallantly plunged into her rescue, and brought her in safety to the shore.

Issue of March 14, 1854

A rencontre took place at the Tunnel in Pickens District, S. C. as we learn from the Keowee Courier, on the 25th ult., between MOSES HOLLIS, a citizen of Pickens District, and JOSEPH PARKER of North Carolina, in which the latter received two stabs in the back, causing almost instant death. HOLLIS has been lodged in jail to await his trial, and the whole affair will in a few weeks undergo judicial examination.

A Female Reporter – The Washington correspondent of the New York Express mentions as an evidence of the progress of the Women's Rights cause, that MRS. PAULINA W. DAVIS, of the Providence Una, (a Woman's Rights paper) has been assigned a seat in the reporters' gallery of the United States Senate. The husband of MRS. DAVIS is a member of the House.

$20 Reward – Runaway from the subscriber on the 13th February, a negro boy named LEROY, about 23 years of age, 5 feet 5 or 6 inches high, weighing about 150 lbs., of a dark copper color, bushy head and whiskers, rather a Roman nose. He is supposed making his way to South Carolina. I will give a reward of twenty dollars for the delivery of him to me near Montpelier Springs, Monroe county, or I will give fifteen dollars to any person who may lodge him in Jail that I may get him.

JOHN MCCALLUM

Death of President WITTICH- We learn that the Rev. L. L. WITTICH, the worthy and efficient President of the Madison Female College, died in that place on Wednesday last. His death may justly be considered a public calamity...

Runaway – From the subscriber, on the night of the 4th instant, a negro boy named UNION, aged about twenty years, stout, well grown, bright mulatto, about six feet high, his left hand has a scar of a burn upon it; he also carried off a common sized bay horse, saddle and bridle. The horse has some white on one of his hind feet, and a small white spot on his forehead, he is about seven years old and rides well. I will give a liberal reward for either or both.

JOSEPH CARRUTHERS

<u>Issue of March 28, 1854</u>

Died – In this city, on the 22nd instant, after a long and painful illness, MR. JOHN GAVAN, of Dalton, Ga. Aged about 39 years.

In Fort Valley, Ga., February 25th, Rev. J. C. POSTELL. Aged 65 years and three days.

$20 Reward – Runaway from the subscriber, on the 20th instant, his indentured apprentice boy, ANDREW TOLLIARD, 18 years of age, of Irish birth, about 5 feet 6 inches high, looks down when spoken to, dark hair, works at the Tin business. I will give the above reward for his delivery in Savannah, and pay Railroad expenses. This is to notify all persons not to harbor or employ him.

Issue of April 4, 1854

Suicide from Jealousy – A woman by the name of PUTNAM, wife of WM. B. PUTNAM, proprietor of a drug store in Philadelphia, committed suicide on Monday last, on account of jealousy of a servant girl who her husband had in his employ. She took poison.

A duel has been fought near Washington City, between MR. CUTTINGS, of New York, and MR. BRECKENRIDGE, of Kentucky, in which it is said the latter was slightly wounded in the neck. The difficulty grew out of some words used in debate.

Trial for Murder – A singular trial for murder occurred in New Orleans on the 19th ultimo, MR. JAMES PATTEN met Col. WALTER TURNBULL, Master Warden of the Port of New Orleans, as he was entering an omnibus in Tehouperoulan street and shot him. PATTEN was tried for murder, his counsel interposed the plea of insanity. He rose in court, denounced his counsel for the subterfuge, declared he was not insane, and that he must be acquitted or convicted upon the ground of justification which he had given to his counsel. The Court permitted him to dismiss his counsel. No ground of justification was maintained and the prisoner was convicted.

Died – In Lee county on the 21st ult. of Typhoid Fever, MRS. EDITH B. MCCLENDON, daughter of JOHN G. and MARY S. RAINES, in the 31st year of her age. She died as she lived – a Christian – nutured in the fear and admonition of the Lord, she never departed there from. A disconsolate husband and three little orphan children mourn her irreplaceable loss.

Death Bed Confession of Murder – A shocking murder of a young German was perpetrated on the Battery in New York some two years since, at a late hour of the night and the case was investigated by Coroner IVES but no clue to the affair was obtained. The mayor offered a reward of $500 for the murderer's apprehension but it had no affect and every idea of arresting the assassin was abandoned. The N. Y. Times, however, says that a few days ago a notorious convict known as "FRENCH", who was arrested with the two murderers, SAUL and HALETT, died in the Sing Sing prison. A few moments before the poor wretch breathed his last, he confessed to a keeper that the murder was committed by SAUL, HOWLETT, JOHNSON (now in State prison) and himself for the paltry sum of $35, which they stole from the corpse and then pitched it over the railing near Castle Garden.

Death of THOMAS NOON TALFOUND – The advices by the steamer Franklin announce the sudden death of this distinguished scholar and jurist which took place on the 12th of March while delivering a charge to the grand jury at Stafford, England...

Death of JOHN B. RAGLAND, junior editor of this paper.

Issue of April 18, 1854

The wife of JOEL WILLIFORD, who was recently _____ bitten by a cat, died in Buffalo of hydrophobia, a few days since.

Killed by a Rattlesnake – We regret, says the Tampa (Fla.) Herald, of the 22d ult., to record the death of MRS. LONG, wife of NATHANIEL LONG, residing on Frog Creek, about sixteen miles south of this place, and near the Altifid. The circumstances attending the melancholy event are as follows: Her husband was in the woods near by getting shingles, and she desirous of calling him home to dinner, walked around so as to call him, and in stepping over a log was bitten in the leg. Her husband carried her home, where she died in a few hours. She was only nineteen years of age.

Issue of April 25, 1854

MISS MARY J. REYNOLDS has been appointed Light House Keeper at Biloxi, Miss. At $400 per annum.

Death of Judge STURGIS – Intelligence reached Columbus last week of the death of the Hon. JOS. STURGIS, who expired in Washington City on the 17th instant. His health had been in a declining state for some time, and during his service as Senator, his decease was daily expected for several weeks. Judge S. has occupied several offices of distinction in our State, including those of Judge of the Superior Court, Senator from Muscogee, and Claim Agent at Washington; and in all these positions was considered a man of superior talents and ability.

Death of DR. SINGLETON – We regret to learn, through a friend, of the death of Dr. JOSEPH J. SINGLETON, late Senator from Lumpkin county. He died of apoplexy, at his residence in Dahlonega, on the 10th inst... Sav. Courier

The Grand Jury of Wilkinson county, at the late sitting of the Superior Court, found a true bill against MCCARDEL, the late clerk, who was charged with burning the Court House. Unable to give bail in the amount required, he is now in jail to await his trial.   Sav. News

Married – In Jones county, on Sunday morning, 16th instant, by JAMES G. BARNES, Esq., MR. W. A. ABANATHA, formerly of North Carolina, to MISS VICTORIA ROSS.

Issue of May 2, 1854

In Habersham county last week, JOHN W. MARTIN was sentenced to the Penitentiary for life, for the murder of his brother-in-law.

We learn from the Thomasville Watchman, that PEYTON WALDIN was killed by DR. HOLLAND, in that place on the morning of the 21st.

Anniversaries – The annual Sunday School celebration was observed by the children of the various congregations last Saturday. About 11o'clock they marched in procession to the Presbyterian church, where excellent addresses were delivered by each of the following young gentlemen as representative of their respective Schools. Methodist Sunday School, Master FRANK ROSS; Baptist, Master WM. BLUNT; Presbyterian, Master SIDNEY LANIER; Episcopal, Master HENRY PETUR; East Macon, Master ROGER MCCALL. The exercises here were closed by an address from E. TRACY, Esq., after which, the Scholars repaired to their respective churches, and finished the festivities of the occasion by disposing of a handsome collection, furnished by the ladies and friends of each congregation.

The trial of MAT WARD, for the murder of Prof. BUTLER is now going on in Elizabethtown, Ky. Hon. J. J. CRITTENDEN and T. F. MARSHALL are engaged in the case.

Married – At the residence of WM. L. HUGHES, by STERLING TUCKER, Esq. MR. ROBERT B. HUGHES to MISS ELIZABETH C. JOHNSON, all of this county.

On the 26th ult., by the Rev. STEPHEN CASTELAW, of Houston county, MR. ISAAC HAYDEN, of Atlanta, to MISS MARY E. daughter of STEPHEN WOODARD, Esq., of Bibb co.

Died – At Fort Valley on Monday, the 28th April, MARTHA THOMAS, only daughter of HENRY G. and MARTHA HARDISON, aged 5 years, two months and fourteen days.

Death of Prof. WILSON – The death of JOHN WILSON, familiarly known as "KIT NORTH", is one of the items of news brought by the Arctic…JOHN WILSON was born at Palsley in 1789. In 1820 he was made Professor of Moral Philosophy in the University of the Scottish Metropolis…

EDWARD STIFF, SR. late editor of the "Radical Reformer", committed suicide in Centre, Ala. On the 23d ultimo, by taking 10 grains of morphine.

Issue of May 16, 1854

Married – At the residence of MR. TODD, SR., in Jones county, on Wednesday evening 10th inst., by D. R. ANDREWS, Esq., MR. ROBT. E. WRIGHT, of Monroe county, Ga., to MISS SARAH ANN STEPHENS, of the former place.

Issue of May 23, 1854

Terrible Steamboat Explosion on the Delaware - Last night about 11 o'clock, the steam towboat was coming down the Delaware near Bordentown, with a number of canal boats in tow, when a boiler exploded with a tremendous report, and with fatal effect. The scalding steam pervaded the deck of the boat, blinding those who were not killed outright, and creating a frightful confusion...WM. WHITE, one of the firemen, was so dreadfully scalded that he died in a very short time. A colored man, who was also employed as a fireman, was very badly scalded, but will, it is thought recover. Three of the sufferers, named WM. EPPEHEIMER, ALEXANDER WILLIAMS, and MARTIN O'MEALLY, were put on board the steamer Thos. Reaney, for the purpose of being brought to the city. O'MEALLY, died in great agony while on the road to the city. The total killed and missing, so far as ascertained, is seven.

WM. TELL Outdone – Extraordinary Pistol Shooting – The New Orleans Picayune gives the following account of an extraordinary exhibition of skill and temerity which took place near that city. The great match and bet of one thousand dollars to eight hundred, has at last been decided, MR. TRAVIS winning the money upon the first shot. The affair came off on May Day, at the private residence of MR. C A. BABBITT, at Bayou Rancos, on Tiger Island, Parish of St. Mary's, in this State. It being difficult to procure an apple, a small orange, about five inches in circumference was substituted. After the shooting distance of thirty-six feet, was measured, and all parties agreed, the orange was placed by the Judges upon the head of a gentleman, a friend of both parties, MR. J. P. O., and no object intervening, the first shot told the story, hitting the orange, half of the bullet going through.
Both gentlemen displayed great nerve upon the exciting ocassion. Some of the best sportsmen and acknowledged best shots in the country were present, and all express themselves fully satisfied that MR. TRAVIS is the best pistol shot in the world.

A Miracle of the present day – Many readers may remember the appearance of MR. JOSEPH BALCH of Johnston, N. Y. in the procession which met DANIEL WEBSTER on his last public entrance into Boston. MR. BALCH was born Feb. 16, 1760, and is now in the ninety-fifth year of his age. He was three years a soldier in the war of the American Revolution, and has been an active participator in all political events since that time. He belongs to a family of singular tenacity of life, and last year he lost by death two sisters, one of whom was one hundred years old, the other was ninety-seven, and both were older than himself. He is now in the possession of all his natural faculties, can read the finest print of the books of the day without spectacles, can walk two miles at a time with most young men, and his memory not only covers very closely all the events of his youth, but keeps pace with the current movements of modern times.

This fine old American gentleman has recently made a visit to Wisconsin and some other parts of the West, in order to see the progress of the country with which he was so well acquainted in its infancy.   Boston Cour.

Death of MARQUIS OF ANGLESEY – The death of WILLIAM HENRY PAGET, first Marquis of Anglesey, has been announced. The deceased was the eldest son the third EARL OF UXBRIDGE, was born in May 1768, and was consequently 86 years of age...

Died – In this city on the 15th instant, MRS. MARTHA ANN CAREY, in the ____th year of her age.

In Barnesville, on the 15th instant, THOMAS W. HARRIS, in the 42nd year of his age.

<u>Issue of May 30, 1854</u>

Married – At the residence of OLIVER WELBORN, Esq., on the 21st inst., by the Rev. JAS. ROQUEMON, MR. BOLING G. MORRIS of Houston, to MISS HENRIETTA ALDRIDGE, of Jones county.

Died – At the residence of PETER SOLOMON, Esq. in Vineville, on the evening of the 25th last, MR. LARKIN GRIFFIN, for many years a worthy and highly esteemed citizen of Macon, aged 55.

Issue of June 6, 1854

On the 27th ult., a recontre took place between THOMAS SEAG, and DR. O'FERRELL, in Appling, Columbia county. O'FERRELL was stabbed through the heart five times.

We learn from the Constitutionalist, that REUBEN SAMUELS who murdered REUBEN SOUTHERLIN, in Stokes county, N. C., was arrested in Knox county, Ky. On the 23d ult. He was followed and captured by JOSEPH B. RAMSEY, Deputy Marshal of Augusta.

LUKE WEST, the celebrated negro-delineator, died a few days ago in Boston. "He was a fellow of infinite jest and most excellent fancy."

The Mayoress of Washington, two hours after the peal of cannon announcing the passage of the Nebraska bill, gave birth to twins, which, she declared, shall be called KANSAS and NEBRASKA.

The wife of THOMAS F. MEAGHER, Esq. the distinguished Irish exile, died recently in Ireland, where she was on a visit.

Issue of June 13, 1854

Among the newly appointed cadets to the U. S. Military Academy at West Point, we notice the following from Georgia: LE ROY NAPIER and E. RUTHERFORD.

Died – In Perry, Ga., on Tuesday May the 9th, MR. WASHINGTON SPIER, in the fifty-sixth year of his age.

Issue of June 20, 1854

The marriage of MRS. ANNA CORA MOWATT and WM. F. RITCHIE, took place yesterday, at Ravenswood, in the presence of an immense concourse. (long article)

Notice - $10 Reward – Runaway from the undersigned on the 6th inst. a negro man named PATTERSON, known by the name of PAT. Said negro is about 5 feet 10 inches high, dark complexion, quite fleshly. I will pay the above reward for his delivery in the Jail of Bibb county.

H. F. REDDING

W. W. HARE, Esq. a distinguished merchant of Charleston, died in the city on Tuesday last.

Died – In this city, on the 16th inst., of Scarlet Fever, GABRIELLA AUGUSTA, only child of THOMAS D. and FRANCES A. KINDER, aged three years.

In Houston county, on the 15th inst., MRS. HARDISON, consort of Hon. JAMES W. HARDISON. She has left a husband, three children and a large number of relatives and friends, to mourn their loss.

Death of SONTAG – HENRIETTE SONTAG, the Queen of Song is dead...died of cholera, on the 18th ult., in the city of Mexico. (long article)

A German, named ANDREW GOETZ, who buried his wife in Union Cemetery, near Williamsburg, about three weeks ago, on Thursday, the 21st ult., blew his brains out with a pistol, while sitting on her grave.

MR. J. C. MEEKS, for a number of years the managing agent of the American Sunday School Union in New York, died on the 22d ult.

Col. KIKKLEY, of Fort Erie, N. Y. a veteran of the war of 1812, in which he performed much valuable service, died of cholera on the 20th ult.

Died – On the 24th June, ALBERT D. eldest son of STEPHEN SLOCUMB, Esq. of this county, aged 8 years, 9 months and 19 days. The deceased was drowned in Echeconnee Creek, near Dickson's Mill in this county.

Issue of July 18, 1854

Died – On Saturday the 15th inst., at the residence of MR. REDDING, in Monroe county, MR. JOHN POWERS, (father of the Hon. A. B. POWERS, of this city) in the 72nd year of his age.

In this city on Sunday the 16h inst., DR. CHARLES S. THOMPSON, of Consumption, in the 47th year of his age.

Upon the same day, a few minutes before the death of her father, DR. CHAS. S. THOMPSON, MISS MARY THOMPSON, aged 13 years.

In Jones county, Ga., on the evening of the 7th of July inst., in the 18th year of her age, MISS TEMPY E. BASS, daughter of BURRELL and MARY BASS. The deceased left her father and mother and two brothers and three sisters, to mourn her departure.

Died in Dooly county, on the 19th day of June last, MRS. MARY E. JONES, consort of the late DONALD B. JONES. The subject of this notice was born in Orangeburg, South Carolina, on the 17th day of January, 1796, and at the age of twelve years, embraced religion and united herself to the Methodist Episcopal church. (long article)

Issue of July 25, 1854

Singular Case of Lockjaw – We learn from the Norristown (Pa.) Watchman, that a short time age a person by the name of JOSEPH DETTRA was employed by MR. WAMPOLE of Towamenetin, in that county, to sow guano and ashes, which caused his fingers to become very sore, and several of the nails to come off. In due time, however, the wounds healed over, and nothing more was thought of it, until about two weeks ago, when, owing, perhaps to the warm weather, he was seized with a great pain in his throat and jaws, and on the 15th inst., died of lock-jaw.

Arrest of An American in Montreal – About a year ago a slave, named OSBORN, belonging to MR. JOHN CAMPBELL, of Maryland, being employed at Cincinnati, took a notion to run off and go to Canada, but was soon anxious to return, and wrote to his master to allow him to come back to his service. MR. CAMPBELL took no notice of the request until lately, when MR. OTT, of Kentucky, a friend of his, set out on a visit to Canada. He requested MR. OTT, if he saw OSBORN, to tell him he would pay his expenses back. MR. O. found him in Montreal, in the employ of a MR. STEVENS, a merchant, and took him aside to speak to him, when up came about half a dozen officers to MR. OTT, who said, "You are our prisoner." MR. OTT requested permission to speak to a friend. The reply was "No Sir – come on". Accordingly, he walked to her Majesty's court, hat in hand, with an escort, arrived before the two Judges, and asked if he was ready for trial, and a warrant produced, charging him with trying to decoy away a bound servant from MR. STEVENS, at a loss of one hundred and fifty dollars per annum. After a four hours trial, MR. OTT was found guilty, and fined, costs, charges, 5 pounds, 11s 2d, and imprisoned five minutes. The affair, it is stated in a letter in the New York Herald, created much excitement, and was instigated by abolitionists.

Issue of August 1, 1854

Removal of the Main Bone in the Leg of a Boy – JOHN BAJA, a lad of fifteen years of age, son of a widow lady of Allegeany City, had received some six months ago an injury of the right leg, by a fall, in consequence of which the whole shaft of the bone had become decayed. To save the limb DR. WALTER removed last week, while the boy was under the influence of chloroform, the main bone of the leg from the knee to the ankle, by expatrition. Incredible as it may appear to the non-professional that a limb could be saved and be made useful by the removal of the whole of the main bone, still, experience has taught that a new bone will be rapidly regenerated in childhood, and the shape, length and usefulness will be preserved. This is a triumph of modern surgery, thus to save a limb, while it is a blessing to the afflicted to be restored without mutilation. The boy is doing well, free from pain, and his recovery appears to be certain. Pittsburg Jour.

Married – In Oxford, Ga., on the 21st ult., by Bishop ANDREWS, MR. JOHN TURNER of Sparta, a member of the present graduating class of Emory College, to MISS ELLA C., eldest daughter of Bishop GEORGE F. PIERCE.

Issue of August 8, 1854

Professor J. MILTON SAUNDERS, has been arrested in Memphis on a charge of harboring runaway slaves.

The Rev. MR. DULIN, a member of the Baltimore Conference of the Methodist Episcopal Church, died in New York on Friday.

Married – By the Rev. W. Y. ATKINSON, on the 27th ultimo, in Hamilton, Harris county, DR. B. B. GARDNER of Upson county to MISS SUSAN B. GORHAM of the former place.

$200 Reward – Runaway from the subscriber a bright mulatto man, JOHN, calling himself JOHN SHERMAN, about 37 years of age, 5 feet 10 inches high, spare built, slender in his waist but wide across the shoulders, stoops a little and flat in the chest, cheek bones high and face long. He took with him from Montezuma, whence he absconded, a large grey horse and buggy. The horse is 16 hands high, 9 years old, weighing perhaps 1000 pounds. Value $250, marked with harness, a little flea bitten on the neck and ears but dappled on the quarters, a fine goer and has a split or break in the hoof of the right fore foot. The buggy was made by WOOD and TOMLINSON, New York, silvermounted, patent axles, two seasons old, yellow, without top and there is a break 8 inches long in the patent leather of the dash board. He was last seen on the 8th day of July near Montezuma. The boy can read and write and is probably making his way to a free State – The above reward will be paid for the arrest of the boy, if taken out of the State of Georgia or $150 if taken any where in the State and lodged in jail, so that I can get him.

G. F. WARD, Tallahassee

Issue of August 22, 1854

$10 Reward – Runaway from the subscriber on the 7th inst., my negro woman, KIZZIAH. She is about 4 ½ feet high, copper color, high bones around her eyes, eyes deep in her head, speaks quick when spoken to, has a scar under her right eye, she is box ankled and sharp heeled, toes turn a little round to the right and left. When she left my plantation she wore off a log chain and two pad locks, which was put on her for running away. She will change her name, and say she belongs to some person else, she has done it twice before. I will pay the above reward for her in any safe jail or at my plantation in Twiggs county, four miles west of Macon.

S. M. BECKCOM

$100 Reward – The subscriber will give the above reward to any person who will apprehend and deliver to the authorities in Lee county, Georgia, or furnish him or them with any means or information, by which JOHN M. BERTINE can be brought to justice, for the murder of WILLIAM SPENCE, which act was perpetrated by BERTINE on last Monday night. BERTINE is a large well built Irishman, about six feet high, weighing one hundred and eighty pounds and about forty or forty-five years old, has (as well as recollected) light red hair, light eyed (brown), fair complected and very red in the face, has a scar over his left eye brow.

CHARLES SPENCE

Issue of August 29, 1854

The body of CHARLES LORING arrived at Jacksonville by the steamer Welaka, on the 13th inst., and was conveyed to St. Augustine for interment.

It is with pain and sorrow that we announce to the community the death of AUGUSTUS H. GIBSON, Esq. who died in this place on the 22d inst…

$30 Reward – Runaway on the night of the 15th inst., from the residence of Col. ELI S. SHORTER, in Eufaula, my boy

ALFRED, about 12 years old, a bright mulatto, black eyes, straight dark brown hair, spare made, walks pigeon toed. I will give the above reward if he is taken fifteen miles from home and lodged in any jail so that I can get him.

HATCH COOK

Married – MICHAEL MCNAMARA to MISS MARY LOU____, all of this city.

By ARMINIUS WRIGHT, MR. JAMES T. _____ and MISS SARAH V. GREEN, all of Monroe _____.

(There are other marriages but they were too difficult to read).

<u>Issue of September 5, 1854</u>

Affecting Incident – While the 46th Regiment were in rank in the barrack square at Windsor, prior to marching out for conveyence to Southampton, en route to Constantinople, a motherless child, six years old, clung to its father's legs. He was peremptorily ordered to send it away, but resolutely answered, "I will not."   LIEUT. HUTTON, touched with scene, took the child and placed two ten-pound notes in its hand, with the hope that some one would befriend it. This, however, proved unnecessary, for having afterwards made his own mother (who is staying at Windsor) acquainted with the circumstances, she adopted the little fellow in time to give the father an assurance that the child should be well cared for. Bucks Advertiser.

Capt. W. B. PRICE died at Memphis on the 21st inst. of typhoid fever.

WILLIAM B. SHEPHARD, who was hung at San Francisco, on the 30th ultimo, for the murder of HENRY C. DAY, stated in his confession that he reached San

Francisco, from Panama, by acting as second mate of the Ship Marianna, Captain ED PROSSETTER, of Baltimore, in 1850 or 1851. It is said he committed the murder because DAY refused to allow him to marry his daughter, but in his confession he declares his entire innocence.

The Hon. THOMAS CLAYTON, formerly a member of the House of Representatives, and afterwards U. S. Senator from Delaware, and at one time chief justice of the Supreme Court of that state died at New Castle on Monday last, in the 77th year of his age.

A venerable minister of the Gospel, the Rev. LEONARD WOODS, died at Andover, Mass., on Thursday last. He was a Professor of the Theological Seminary of that place, and was in the 85th year of his age.

Half a Century in Bed – The New York Observer states that SUSAN PIERSON, of Bridge____pton, Long Island, died in February last, at the advanced age of seventy-two years, ____fifty-two of which she had not set her feet upon the floor. During that period, the _____ of her travels, with the exception of a _____ spent in a neighbor's house, was from one ____of a room to another, in the arms of _____ strong man. This change was always preceded by a loss of voice, from which she would not recover until a night's repose. The ____ medical skill was unable to restore her ____ or even to enable her to sit up in bed. "____ Suzy", as she was called, was an humble truthful child of God. Knitting was her ____ constant employment, and her Bible was ever by her side. During the entire term of her confinement she received the untiring _____ of a sister, who survives her, and is 80 (?) years of age.

Issue of September 12, 1854

A Duel is reported to have been fought, with broad-swords, at Havana, on the 18th, between SARTORIUS, the postmaster of that city, and GAMUSA, an officer of the customs, in which the p. m. fared badly.

The combatants were parted before, it is believed, any mortal wound was inflicted.

MRS. MARTHA MOORE shot herself while deranged, at Petersburg, on Monday. She had before made several attempts at suicide.

Captain DUFF GREEN died at Falmouth, Virginia, on the 24th ult.

S. T. CHAPMAN, Esq., Editor of the Journal & Courier, fell a victim to the prevailing pestilence in Savannah on Sunday morning...

Married – In Crawford county, on the 7th inst., by the Hon. CULVERHOUSE, HENRY SADIFUR, to MISS MARY HORTMAN, of said county.

Issue of September 19, 1854

Among the deaths from Yellow Fever in Savannah during the past week, we note that of Capt. JONATHAN OLMSTEAD, cashier of the Marine Bank. Capt. OLMSTEAD was an old and highly respected citizen of Savannah, and died universally esteemed in that community.

We regret also to announce the death of Judge W. HARRIS, in the same place and from the same disease. He was an old citizen of Macon, and leaves many friends among us who will hear of his decease with great sorrow. His partner, MR. THOS. A. BROWN, is now dangerously ill of the same disorder.

JOHN N. BRADY, Esq. a lawyer in New York, was so severely beaten by a gang of rowdies, a few days since, that he died on Friday morning. It appears that MR. BRADY was returning home in company with his landlord, MR. MCBRIDE, last on Saturday night last, when on reaching Mott street, they met a gang of rowdies, about twelve in number, who immediately made an attack upon them. MR. BRADY was severely beaten, and among other wounds, his spine was injured. After considerable difficulty, he and his friend escaped from the ruffians and went home. Immediately after entering the house, MR. BRADY became weak and helpless, and remained in a suffering condition till death ensued. No policeman appeared during the attack, although the police was loudly called for, and the assailants escaped. The deceased leaves a wife and children.

A young man named SHORT, clerk in a dry goods store in Cincinnati, and a young lawyer named PEACOCK, from Chicago, fought a duel in Kentucky on Monday. On the second round, SHORT was fatally wounded in the left breast. They fought about a young girl to whom SHORT was engaged.

The mother of Senator FISH, died in New York on Wednesday morning, aged 80 years. She was the widow of Col. NICHOLAS FISH, a gallant officer in the United States Army, and one of the old Knickerbockers. MRS. FISH was a lineal descendant of Governor STUYVESANT, and has lived, herself, to the good old age of four score years.

A dispatch from Philadelphia, dated the 7th inst., says: Lieut. EDWARD C. LEWIS, formerly of the Pennsylvania Volunteers in Mexico, who was arrested on Friday last charged with numerous forgeries of land warrants, was held in $2500 bail, but failing to appear for a hearing yesterday and to-day, his bail has been forfeited.

Capt. JOHN PLEASANTS died suddenly in Norfolk on Tuesday of bilious cholic.

The Princess ZENAIDE CHARLOTTE JULIE BONAPARTE, died at Naples on the 8th. She was the eldest daughter of JOSEPH BONAPARTE, King of Spain, and was born in Paris on July 8th, 1802. She married her cousin, Prince CHARLES, eldest son of LUCIAN BONAPARTE, and leaves by him eight children. Her usual residence was Rome, where three of her married daughters and her eldest son, Prince MUSSIGNANO, are now living.

Married – On the 13th inst., by STERLING TUCKER, Esq. MR. ASA SMITH to MISS MARGIANIA ARTHUR, all of this county.

On the evening of the 13th inst. by Rev. G. H. HANCOCK, DANIEL CULVER, to MISS CAROLINE E. RUSH, all of Macon.

Died – At the residence of his father, on the 5th inst., of typhoid fever, THOMAS G. son of W. F. and AGNES WILLIAMS, of Pike county, Ga. The deceased was a young man in the 23d year of his age...leaving a kind father, an affectionate mother, and a broken-hearted wife and child and brothers and sisters...

Issue of September 26, 1854

Report of the Sexton – During the week ending on Saturday the 23d inst., there were eight deaths. On the 17th JERRY, a negro man from Monroe co., sent here for medical attention – disease, consumption. 18th – ABRUM, negro man, 40 years, bilious fever. Also, JACOB MASTICK from Savannah. 19th –negro man, ADAM, 60 years, consumption. 20th – negro child, 2 years old, disease unknown, 21st – GILBERT MCSWAIN, from Savannah, yellow fever. ____DOYLE, from Savannah, yellow fever. FANNIE W. WALLAN, from Savannah, 2 years, inflammation of the brain.

We have received from an esteemed friend in Crawford county, a tribute of respect to the memory of DR. WM. HALES, a young gentleman of much promise, who lately died in Savannah, of the prevailing epidemic.

September 18, 1854, 5 o'clock P.M. The Board of Health – 2 deaths from yellow fever during the last 24 hours. JAMES KELLY, aged 28 years, Ireland. MRS. HART, 25 years, England.

Sept. 19, 4 o'clock, P.M. MRS. ____JACKSON, aged 55 years. PANTLEON SIMON, aged 40 years. MARGARET SINTAPOWER, aged 70 years.

A Navy Captain Cashiered – We learn that Captain SAMUEL W. DOWNING, of the U. S. Navy, who was recently tried by a general naval court-martial, at Philadelphia, was found guilty of all the charges preferred against him, with the exception of the charge of "disobedience of orders", and sentenced to be cashiered. The finding and sentence of the Court having been approved by the President of the United States, Capt. DOWNING has been notified that he will no longer be regarded as an officer of the Navy.

Death of an Old Printer – JOHN WAIT, an old and respected Printer, died in this city yesterday, of jaundice, making the seventh member of the craft who bowed the heads in death during the present sickly season among us. MR. WAIT, was 66 years of age, and was born in England, where he learned his trade. Some years since he emigrated to this country, and latterly resided in Savannah, continuing up to the time of his death, his vocation as Compositor in our morning paper offices. He was at the close of the publication of the Sun in this city some years since, a copartner in the concern. Industrious in habits, and cheerful in deportment , he won many friends among his acquaintances. Republican, 21st inst.

Issue of October 3, 1854

Death of JAS. G. GOULD, Esq. - It becomes our duty to chronicle the melancholy intelligence of the death of this worthy young man, which occurred at Marietta, on Thursday last.

Death of JAMES RHIND - ...cashier of the Branch of the State Bank in this city. He expired at his residence on the Sand Hills, on Monday morning.
Augusta Constitutionalist

Death of Col. J. W. JACKSON – The Hon. JOSEPH W. JACKSON of Savannah, expired of yellow fever in that city, on Thursday last, in the 58th year of his age...

Death of Gen. HARALSON - ...of Troup county. He expired in LaGrange on Tuesday, the 26th ult.

DR. J. C. PATTERSON, charged with robbing the mails, has been found guilty in the U.S. Court in Nashville, Tenn.

The New Orleans riots have entirely ceased. JOHN KANE, one of the men supposed to have been killed, has since been found. He was shot four times, but may recover from his wounds.

A collision occurred on the Georgia Rail Road on Thursday night, below Camak, between the up passenger train and a ____ freight train, by which the engineer on the train, ROBERT SPENCER, and a fireman named CHARLES MARSH were instantly killed, and ____DORSEY, engineer, and THOMAS GIBSON, fireman on the down train, were seriously injured. JOHN BALDWIN, machinist, was badly scalded. A negro, belonging to one of ____ trains, was also slightly injured.

Pension Forger Convicted – Wm. M. MOORE, according to advices received at the Pension Bureau has been convicted before the United States Court at Nashville, Tenn., under an indictment for fraud and forgery in preparing papers in a revolutionary pension case, on which he obtained no money from the Treasury, his crimes being detected before final adjudication on the case. He had been twelve years a magistrate, was a merchant by profession, and has a wife and eight children.

Obituary – Died in the city of Savannah, of the prevailing epidemic, after an illness of five days, MR. WILLIAM A. HALEE, formerly of Knoxville, Ga., in the 23rd year of his age...

Died near Marion, Twiggs county, on the morning of the 26th September, HENRY HARTWELL, youngest son of LEWIS and LUCY ANN F. SOLOMON, aged 14 months.

Died in this city, on the 26th ult., MRS. ELIZABETH J. ALLEY, wife of F. H. ALLEY, aged 35 years 11 months and 1 week. MRS. ALLEY was a native of Charleston, S.C...member of the Baptist Church.

<u>Issue of October 10, 1854</u>

Murder – On Saturday, the 30th ult., PETER CURRY, a son of one of our oldest citizens, received twenty-four stabs from the hands of one LUKE NOWELL, from the effects of which he died on the following Tuesday. The affair occurred at night in the Warrior District of this county, and as far as we can learn, in the following manner: NOWELL, CURRY, and others were attending at a 'corn shucking' at the house of one of their neighbors, when one of the party proposed to go to a corner of the fence where a bottle of liquor was secreted, and there take a dram. While there NOWELL became excited, and for some cause or other, drew a knife upon CURRY, but was compelled to desist. Shortly afterwards, CURRY becoming greatly intoxicated, drew off into a corner and fell asleep. The party soon broke up, leaving CURRY behind them. NOWELL and one other went down the road – the balance of the party in another direction. These last soon heard cries, and returning observed NOWELL striking repeatedly at CURRY, who was on the ground. On pursuit, NOWELL, it is said, threw away his knife, which was afterwards found and identified. It was very bloody. Upon examining CURRY it was found that twenty-four stabs had been inflicted on his body. NOWELL was arrested and committed to jail on Sunday, and now awaits his trial at the next term of the Superior Court.

MRS. HARRIS, daughter of Gov. TROUPE, of Georgia, and wife of Lieut. HARRIS, U.S.N. was dreadfully burned, at the Sweet Springs, Va., a short time since, in endeavoring to extinguish the flames which had caught the curtain of her chamber from a candle.

<u>Issue of October 17, 1854</u>

From the Louisville Courier – Horrible Murder – Man Killed by his Overseer and Wife. We were informed yesterday evening by passengers on the cars from Lexington, of a tragedy that occurred in the county of Fayette, on Saturday night, which almost transcends belief, it is of so horrible a nature. MR. FRAZER, a farmer of the county, had been absent with stock at New York for several months, and on Saturday telegraphed his family that he would reach home that evening. His neighbor and partner, MR. CASTLEMAN, awaited his arrival at the depot and conveyed him to his residence. Leaving the house, MR. C.was startled about an hour afterwards by the report of a gun. He immediately went to FRAZER's and there discovered him dead, the house darkened, MRS. F. above stairs, GRIGG, the overseer, below, and a daughter, aged eleven, with the mother. They accounted for the death of the man by the accidental discharge of a shotgun, which he had in his hand preparing to shoot a rat. Suspicions were aroused and the overseer and MRS. FRAZER both arrested. The body of the deceased was terribly bruised, a hole shot through his head, another through his body, his throat was badly cut, and three ribs broken, effects not reasonably caused by accident.

There appeared to be no doubt in the minds of those advised of the facts, as to the criminality of MRS. FRAZER and GRIGG. Previous to this time the neighbors had suspected improper intimacies between the two, and it is supposed that it was for the purpose of getting FRAZER out of the way, so as to render a marriage feasible, that the awful deed was accomplished. There are various circumstances connected with the affair, which go to criminate the suspected parties. During Monday and yesterday they were undergoing preliminary trial.

Dreadful Double Murder and Suicide (N. Y. Tribune), Greene, Chenango co., Oct 5. I have the unpleasant duty of giving you an account of one of the most horrible double murders and suicides that has ever come to my notice, committed about four miles east of his village, and the turnpike leading to Coventry. It appears that one DAVID D. DAVIS, a returned Californian, (the murder and suicide) had a misunderstanding with his wife and lately separated, they the past summer living apart, and I believe both parties had commenced actions for divorce. The trials were to come off next week. The immediate cause of the whole difficulty, I understand, was jealousy. This afternoon DAVIS met his brother-in-law, BUEL

HOTCHKISS, (at whose house his wife had been boarding) at the house of a MR. GILMORE, a near neighbor and after conversation, HOTCHKISS withdrew a revolver and shot him, killing him instantly. He then ran to his brother-in-law's house and shot his wife, mortally wounding her, and then shot himself through the heart.

Married – In Crawford county, on the evening of the 12th inst., by the Rev. S. W. BURNETT, DR. ADOLPHUS PURIFOY of Bibb and MRS. HENRIETTA BOON of Crawford county, Georgia.

Obituary – Died in this city, of Bilious Fever, on Monday the 16th inst., WILLIAM COLLINS, in the 46th year of his age.

Issue of October 24, 1854

Marriages listed but to dim to read

Mob-law Violence – DAVE THOMAS who was found guilty of murder in the second degree by the court of Caroline county, Maryland, was forcibly taken from jail, on Saturday night by the indignant populace of Denton, and hung until he was dead. The Baltimore Patriot says: "This is first instance of Lynch law that has occurred in Maryland of which we have any knowledge." THOMAS was a negro.

Issue of October 31, 1854

A Wife Killed by her Husband – We understand that a man by the name of BIRD FOWLER, living about two miles from this city, shot his own wife on last Friday night. At the time we are writing, the unfortunate woman still lives, but her wound is considered mortal. FOWLER was arrested, and is now confined in the county jail.

Escape of a Prisoner – We notice in our Columbus Exchanges, that WRIGHT – the man held in Jail to answer the charge of murdering the Deputy Sheriff of Muscogee – has effected his escape from prison. JACK BOYD was tried and convicted for the same offence, at a late term of the Superior Court, but remains in Jail to await the action of our Supreme Judges. WRIGHT, we believe, is the party who actually committed the killing, and from all the circumstances we have learned, we should say he acted very discreetly in taking leave of the good people of Columbus. The Sheriff of Muscogee, has offered a reward of $500 for the apprehension of WRIGHT.

A duel on the Elysian Fields at Hoboken – New York, Oct. 19. The Evening Post states that a duel was fought on the Elysian Fields at Hoboken this morning, where HAMILTON and BURR fought, between PETER THOMPSON, of South Carolina, and a MR. HORTON, of this city. They fought at fifteen paces with pistols, and at the second fire South Carolina received the ball of New York in his left arm, causing a painful wound. The particulars of the difficulty are not stated, but it is announced that they shook hands, and expressed themselves satisfied.

<u>Issue of November 7, 1854</u>

The Warrenton, Virginian Whig says: EASTER, a negro woman, the property of MRS. ELIZA F. CARTER, near Upperville, in Fauquier county, died on the 17th July, having attained the age of one hundred and forty years! This is one of the most remarkable cases of longevity on record.

W. W. FARMER, Lieutenant Governor of Louisiana, died in New Orleans, on Sunday the 29th ult., of yellow fever.

Married – In this city, on Wednesday last, by the Rev. EUSTACE SPEAR, Col. I. D. N. JOHNE and MISS MARY C. HAMMOND, all of this city.

The trial of STEPHEN J. BEALE, dentist, at Philadelphia, charged with violating the person of a young woman, has been concluded – the jury having rendered a verdict of guilty. His counsel immediately moved for a new trial.

Issue of November 14, 1854

EDWARD Z. C. JUDSON, alias, NED BUNTLINE, who was arrested a few days since for shooting a colored man, at Bath, Maine, has been acquitted on the ground that he committed the act in self defense.

Married – On the 25th ultimo, by the Rev. MR. MADDOX, DR. W.A. WRIGHT to MISS MARY BANDY, all of Pike county.

On the 7th inst., by the Rev. WILLIAM CRAWFORD, MR. JOHN BROWN of Monroe county to MRS. H. RODGERS of Upson county.

In Columbus, on the 7th inst., by the Rev. MR. DALZELL, Capt. JAMES M. BIVINS of this city to MISS MARY FRANCES DRUMRIGHT of Columbus.

Fatal Duel – Columbus, Nov. 9 – A duel was fought today fourteen miles from this city, between PETER GRAFFREY and DR. DUNCAN W. RAY. The former was killed upon the second fire, while the latter remained unhurt.

Issue of November 21, 1854

We are called upon this morning to announce the death of one our oldest and most respectable citizens, Capt. JOHN HUNTER, at the age of eighty-seven years...

The remains of the Hon. WILLIAM T. BARRY, a distinguished citizen of Kentucky, and formerly Minister Plenipotentiary to Spain from the United States, and Postmaster General, and who died in England in 1835, were recently carried to Frankfort, Ky., to be interred in the capital cemetery.

Obituary – Died at his residence in Crawford county, on the 10th of October last, of Typhoid Dysentery, Rev. DOLPHIN DAVIS, in the sixty-third year of his age. The deceased was a native of North Carolina and emigrated to this State when seventeen years old. He had been a member of the Methodist Episcopal Church about thirty-nine years, more than twenty-five of which, he served as a licensed and ordained preacher.

Married – On the morning of the 16th inst., by the Rev. D. MYRICK, Col. EDMUND BLOUNT, of Clinton, Ga., to MISS LUCY E., daughter of the Rev. JONES E. COOK, late of Rome, Ga.

In Jasper county, on Wednesday the 8th instant, by the Rev. MR. HENDERSON, Col. GEORGE A. BROWN, of Americus and MISS GEORGIA V., daughter of J. HOLLAND, Esq. of that county

In Knoxville, on the 8th inst., MR. THOS. CRUTCHFIELD, JR. to MISS S. E. OLIVER.

On the 9th of November, by the Rev. JOSEPH T. SMITH, MR. WILLIAM H. WEEDEN to MISS AUGUSTA ANN RENFRO – all of Sandersville.

Issue of November 28, 1854

Died – On the 13th inst., MARIA THERESE, eldest daughter of J. M. BOARDMAN, aged three years, three months and eighteen days.

Married – On the 22d inst., by the Rev. EBENEZER JOINER, Esq., MR. PATRICK H. HOLT of Houston county to MRS. IRINA HOLT of Crawford county.

$100 Reward – Ranaway from the subscriber, about ten weeks since, his negro man JIM, twenty-two years of age, about six feet high, and weighs 180 pounds, his right leg is 1 ½ inches shorter than his left, dark complexion. JIM, was bought from MR. M EVERETT, near Macon, Ga., and no doubt lurking about the City of Macon, if he has not been decoyed off by some white man. A reward of twenty-five dollars will be paid for the boy JIM if delivered to me, or lodged in any Jail so that I can get him, and if the said boy has been stolen, a reward of $100 will be given for the thief with proof to convict. Address the subscriber at Magnolia Post Office, Macon county, Ala.

GEORGE W. SAYERS

Issue of December 5, 1854

Surgical Operation – An interesting case of excision of a portion of the lower jaw-bone was performed a few days since, by DR. FRED GEDDINGS, before the students of the Medical College. The patient was a negro girl, about 14 years old. After dissection the flap of the cheek, he divided the bone in two places, removing a section of about two inches in length. No chloroform was administered, yet the patient continued calm and quiet during the whole operation, which has ever been regarded one of the most painful in surgery. It lasted about five minutes, and was performed in a manner highly creditable to the operator.
Ch. Mercury

Death of MR. P. M. JUDSON

Married – In Jones county, on the morning of the 26th inst., at the house of NATHANIEL J. GLOVER, by JOHN JARRELL, Esq., DR. BENJAMIN W. FINNEY, of Gordon, and MISS CAROLINE M. daughter of WILLIAM REYNOLDS Esq., of Jones county.

Died – On the 28th ult., MILLIE PIERPONT, infant daughter of MR. and MRS. J. M. BOARDMAN.

Funeral Notice – The friends and acquaintances of the late P. M. JUDSON are requested to attend the funeral services, which will take place, this day at 3o'clock, at the Lanier House. Particular notice is given to the I. O. O. F. of which he was known to be a member.

$100 Reward – Ranaway or was stolen from me on the 5th of October, a negro boy named PETER, of light complexion, down cast look, spare built and weighing about 130 or 140 pounds. When he looks up, he shows a great deal of the white of his eye. A liberal reward will be given for his safe delivery, or apprehension in jail, and for the conviction of the thief I will give one hundred dollars.

ELIZA S. COTTON

Issue of December 12, 1854

Married – On the 7th inst., by Rev. S. LANDRUM, in Vineville, at the residence of her father, Col. JAMES DEAN, MISS FRANCES M. DEAN to DR. DAVID R. E. WINN of Americus.

In Crawford county on Thursday 7th inst., by C. H. WALKER, J.P., WILLIAM F. KENNEDY to MISS MARY ANN D. FREE.

Issue of December 19, 1854

THOMAS P. COPE died at his residence in Philadelphia, on Wednesday. He was the originator of COPE's line of Liverpool packets, and for half a century occupied high positions in Philadelphia. He is supposed to be worth about $7,000,000. He was a quaker and commenced business in Philadelphia, his native place, as a tabacconist. His sign then was THOMAS P. COPE, and the advertisement in the papers was 'THOMAS P. COPE sells tobacco in Willing's Alley'. He became at last, a large owner at shipping. The ships Thomas P. Cope, Algonquin, Monongahela, Susquehanna, Philadelphia, and a number of others were his property.

Married – On the 13th inst., at the residence of MRS. SANDERS, by his Honor JOHN H. BRANTLEY, MR. IRWIN J. WOOD to MISS RHODA SANDERS, all of Bibb county.

In Vineville, on the morning of the 14th inst., by Rev. G. H. HANCOCK, THOMAS W. BAXTER, Esq. of Smith county Texas, to MISS ELLENDRA F. SCOTT of the former place.

Issue of December 26, 1854

GEO. W. KENDALL, Esq. of the New Orleans Picayune, we see it stated, has recently taken unto himself a wife. She is a Parisian by birth and the marriage took place at Paris.

Married –On the evening of the 19th inst., by Rev. L. SOLOMON, WILLIAM S. KELLY, Esq. of Twiggs county, to MRS. MARY A. E. CHAPMAN, of the county of Bibb.

On the evening of the 21st inst., by Rev. L. SOLOMON, HENRY F. SOLOMON, Esq. to MISS MARY E. FITZPATRICK, all of Twiggs county.

Issue of January 2, 1855

Homicide – A man named JESSE DANIELS received a blow on the head, from the hands of J. ATTOWAY, at the Factory, on Monday evening, which caused a severe fracture of the skull, and from the effect of which he died in a short time. It seems that there had been some difficulty previously, but DANIEL's friends were leading him away, when ATTOWAY came behind him and struck the blow, which terminated his life...
Augusta Const. 27th ult.

Murder – An Irishman, named SAMUEL WILSON, a painter by trade, and but recently arrived in our city from Charleston, was shot on Sunday evening last by WM. A. ARCHER and almost instantly killed. It appears that ARCHER had some words with the deceased in the Bar Room at the corner of Centre and Broad streets, and struck WILSON with a stick. They then left the House together and when only a few feet from the door, ARCHER drew his pistol and fired, the ball taking effect in his left breast and passed through the chest, lodging near the spine. ARCHER was pursued and arrested at his own house. He is now in jail and will undergo an examination before a Board of Magistrates. Ib.

Death by Violence – We have just received the painful intelligence of the death of two men in Fannin county, by the hand of a MR. GUNTER.
We understand the facts to be as follows: Three men came to MR. GUNTER's house in search of a MR. SMITH, and not finding him, went on their way; but returned in a short time and commenced throwing down GUNTER's fence in order to ride in. GUNTER came out of his still house, which was inside the inclosure and forbid them throwing it down, but they persisted and a fight ensued, and the three being an over match for GUNTER, he retired into the still

house. One of the men whose name was MILLER, and who had fired a (revolver) pistol during the recounter, now rode up to the door of the still house and fired at the door. GUNTER then shot MILLER with a rifle, who fell from his horse and immediately expired. Another one of the combatants by the name of NASH seized the pistol which had fell from MILLER's hands and fired at GUNTER in the door, whereupon GUNTER stepped out with another rifle, seeing which NASH turned and fled, and GUNTER fired at him, he fell and expired in about half hour. MILLER was shot a little below the heart, and NASH in the small of the back.

We derived this information from a gentleman, who heard the testimony on the part of the State, when GUNTER was arrested, who was still a prisoner at last account. As the subject will receive judicial investigation we forbear any comments other than our expression of regret that so much of violence should exist in our country. Dahlonega Signula, 23d inst.

Col. JOHN BLISS, formerly of the U.S. Army, and who participated in the battles of Chippeway and Bridgewater, in the latter of which he was wounded, died lately in Florida.

Married – In this city on the evening of the 21st inst., by Rev. G. H. HANCOCK, MR. S. W. WALKER, and MISS LAURA M. EVANS.

In this city, on the 28th Dec., 1854, by Rev. S. LANDRUM, MR. E. O. WHITTINGTON to MISS FANNIE E. RICHARDSON, all of this city.

In this city, on the 17th inst., by AMOS BENTON, Esq. MR. ORREY ODOM to MISS FRANCIS M. JORDAN – also, on the 20th, MR. G JACKSON WILLIAMS to MISS ELPHANY SHERRY, all of this county.

In this city, on the morning of the 21st ult., by Rev. BOB L. BRECK, MR. WM. T. BROWN, of Americus, Ga. to MISS LUCIA M. TRAPP, of Macon, Ga.

Died – In Vineville, on the afternoon of the 24th inst., of pneumonia, WILLIAM A. DEAN, in the 30th year of his age.

Issue of January 9, 1855

In one of the Connecticut Courts, lately, one JESSE W. ROSS, was on trial on a charge of assault with intent to kill, his counsel being engaged in a plea in his defense, when his client suddenly came upon him and tumbled him over. This was deemed to be conclusive proof of insanity, and the Court ordered that he be provided for in an Insane Asylum.

Married – In Savannah on the evening of the 28th inst. at the residence of JOHN JONES, Esq. by the Rev. W. G. CONNOR of Columbus, WILLIAM F. PLANE, Esq. of Columbus to MISS C. HELEN JOHNSON.

In this city, on the 2d inst., by Rev. S. LANDRUM, MR. FREIDCHRICH SCHLUMGEN to MISS LOUISA KAUF all of Macon.

Issue of January 16, 1855

Singular Accident – The Manchester (N.H.) American says that an infant son of MR. WILLIAM GARDNER, of Mason Village, was strangled on the night of the 25th, in this singular manner. The foot of his little sister, who was in the same bed got entangled in the string of the night dress about the neck of the child, and drew it so tightly as to cause its death.

Married – In this city on the 4th inst., by Rev. S. LANDRUM, MR. WM. A. HARTLY, to MISS MARY L. GROCE, all of this city.

Died – At the residence of WILLIAM S. KELLY, Esq. in Twiggs county, on the morning of the 7th inst. after a painful illness of eight weeks, EUGENIUS S. CHAPMAN, aged four years and four months.

<u>Issue of January 23, 1855</u>

Death of Capt. SAMUEL PHILBRICK – It is with regret that we record the death of Captain SAMUEL PHILBRICK, which took place late on Saturday evening last, at his residence in this city. Capt. P. was an active, energetic citizen...He leaves a wife and three daughters to mourn his irreparable loss. He was a native of New Hampshire, and removed to this State in 1819, since which time he has been closely identified with the commercial interests of out city.
Sav. Cour.

Singular Escape – Not long since, MR. WILLIAM BONNER, JR., of this county, was driving two spirited horses through a long lane on the western part of this county; one of them stumbled and fell against the tongue which broke short off. As they were going down hill, the buggy ran on the horses, which frightened them and they were off quick as thought. The driver jumped out and MR. B. was thrown either out or jumped out; his cloak caught in the axletree, and he was dragged some distance and so severely stunned as to lose his consciousness for awhile. The frightened horses soon overtook MR. and MRS. STOWE of Columbia county, who were in a buggy and could neither turn to the right or left, owing to the deep gully and fence on either side, and what is singular enough, ran over them in such a way as to leave MR. B's buggy pretty much on top of theirs, crushing it up, but leaving them uninjured. Both buggies were badly broken, but no serious injury occurred to either of the parties. MR. BONNER's cloak was found twisted round the axeltree. Sandersville Georgian, Jan. 18

Death of JOHN S. BARBOUR, SR. – We regret to learn that this gentleman died at his residence in Culpepper, on the 12th inst. in the 66th year of his age. He had been a public man for the greater part of his life, had represented his district in Congress for many years, and had also been in the State Legislature...   Richmond Penny Post, 15th

Horrible Calamity – The Poughkeepsie Press of Friday, informs us that on Tuesday morning last a woman named FORD, and her child, aged six years, were burnt to death at Newburg. It appears by the evidence received by the coroner that the mother was a woman of intemperate habits, and that she had retired to bed with her daughter, leaving a lighted candle near her couch. From the candle, undoubtedly by accident, the fire was communicated to the bed-clothes, resulting in the above horrible calamity.

Married – On the 17th inst. by the Rev. W. J. KEITH, MR. JOE E. TAYLOR to MISS JULIA C. WINN, both of Monroe county.

Issue of January 30, 1855

Public Execution – The negro, JOHN, who was convicted of the murder of MARK SWEENEY at the last May term of our Superior Court, suffered the extreme penalty of the law on Friday last.

Homicide – On Sunday night, during the excitement attendant upon the alarm of fire, we are sorry to announce that desparate affray occurred in this city. A young man by the name of GOSS, a bricklayer by trade, received a pistol ball in the pit of the stomach, and no reasonable hope can be entertained of his recovery. Owing to the numberless reports in circulation, it is impossible for us to furnish any reliable statement of the particulars connected with this unfortunate affair. It is known that the shot was fired by WILLIAM A. B. GODDARD, of this city; but, up to the time our paper goes to press, the attendant circumstances have not transpired. GOSS was comparatively a stranger in Macon – having resided here only a few weeks. The police have not succeeded in arresting MR. GODDARD.

Murder by a Negro – MR. GEORGE W. ACKER, who was very well known to our citizens, has met a violent death by a negro wood-cutter. The tidings as they came first from a gentleman, resident of Chastings Bluff, were that MR. ACKER had left his house on Tuesday morning for the avowed purpose of looking after a fellow who he had employed to cut wood, and that shortly after his horse returned alone to the house. Alarmed for his safety, MR. ACKER's friends began to send out and search for him – but in vain: ____ when the negro came home at night they arrested and carried him along on the ____ search. They carefully followed the horse track which led to the spot where the negro had been at work in the morning. Here there were unmistakeable marks of the violent ____ of death, and then the ruffian, TOM, admitted his guilt, and conducted them to the body.

The following confession of the murder appears in the News: TOM says: "When he (MR. ACKER) first came to me, he says, TOM, I don't think you cut wood enough, you don't put it up right, making too many holes; and if you don't cut two cords, I will make you cut two and a half and when MR. ACKER started off, I says to him, MR. ACKER, it seems that I can't please you nohow. He then jumped down from his horse and made ____ me with his sword cane drawn and then I run, thinking he was going to stick it through me. He said, that if I talked that way to him he would stick it through me. I then struck at him with the axe, and hit him over the eye, and he then run and I run after him, and he hollowed, Oh Lord! And when I caught him I dropped the axe, and threw MR. ACKER, down, and MR. ACKER took up the axe and struck me with the axe on the breast. MR. ACKER was in a sitting position at the time he hit me. I then took the axe from him as he was sitting, and when I had the axe drawn, MR. ACKER said to me, if I would not kill him he would not trouble me any more, and if I did kill him, his wife and children would suffer and as he tried to getup, I struck him back of the head a very heavy lick with the edge of the axe. That is the blow that knocked out his brains, and he did not speak or move afterwards. I then looked out a place to bury him where he was found in the run of the branch. No other person saw me, and I did not tell a living soul of it until last night, when we were all looking for him; when I told MR. LADD (?) that I would show him where the body was. I never had any notion to kill any one but ____ of our drivers that we named DENISE, because he wanted to whip me wrongfully." Mobile Register, 18th

Married – In this city, by Rev. S. LANDRUM, on the 23d inst., MR. ROBERT W. SCALES to MISS FANNIE MARTIN, daughter of MRS. E. J. MARTIN.

In this city, on the 25th inst., by Rev. S. LANDRUM, MR. WM. O. HURT to MRS. MARY SAGE.

Issue of February 6, 1855

Death of Bishop CAPERS – It will be perceived with deep regret, from a telegraphic dispatch in our columns this morning, that DR. WILLIAM CAPERS, one of the Bishops of the Methodist Church, South, died at his residence at Anderson, C.H. on Monday morning, in the 66th year of his age. DR. CAPERS was born in St. Thomas Parish, on the

26th of January, 1790. He received the degree of M.A. from the South Carolina College, where he was educated, and was received into the annual Conference of his native State, as a traveling Minister, in 1808. In 1828 he was sent to England as the representative of the American Methodist Episcopal Church to the British Conference, and for several years he was one of the general Missionary Secretaries. In 1846 he was elected Bishop. Charleston Courier

Issue of February 13, 1855

Conviction of a Duelist – JUAN PAGES has been found guilty of manslaughter at New Orleans, with a recommendation to mercy, for killing JUAN PASTER in a duel. The prisoner is about 40 years of age and has a family. The Courier says: "This is the first time in the annals of Louisiana that a conviction for dueling has taken place, although the statutes making the slaying of a man in a duel murder are coeval with the constitution of the State. It is true this duel was fought under the most atrocious circumstances, and in a most murderous manner. Nevertheless, we hail this verdict as an important legal precedent, and as an evidence of a healthy state of public opinion. The duel, it appears, was fought with knives; the parties were equal in physical power, and when one objected to the knife of the other, the latter offered and actually did exchange knives, and with the weapon of his antagonist slew him.

Died – At Fort Gaines, on the 26th ult., Maj. JAMES HOLMES, in the 58th year of his age.

Issue of February 20, 1855

Died – In East Macon, on the 13th inst., in the 23d year of her age, MARY JANE wife of JAMES B. NELSON.

Married – At Christ Church in this city, on the 10th inst., by the Rev. MR. REESE, MR. H. A. TROUTMAN and MISS TABITHA E. NAPIER, both of Vineville.

Issue of February 27, 1855

$500 Reward – General Jail Delivery – Three prisoners who had been confined for some time past in our county jail, effected their escape on last Saturday night, about 8 o'clock. The parties were SAMUEL SCOVILL, charged with the robbery of the Marine bank, LUKE NOWELL charged with the murder of PETER CURRY and one RALEY, charged with negro-stealing in Sumpter county. All of these men were confined in cells in the third story of the Jail, but managed by means of saws, files, and probably skeleton keys, to get down to the first floor, whence they made their egress by picking a large hole through the wall. It is said that NOWELL and RALEY betook themselves to the swamp below the city, but that SCOVILL was carried off in a buggy which was awaiting him just outside of the jail. This, however, is only one of many rumors, nor do we know how much confidence it is entitled to. The Sheriff, MR. THARP, has offered a reward of $500 for their arrest, and is taking every possible step to secure their capture.

Death of D.J. DAVIS. Esq. – It becomes our painful duty to announce the death of MR. DAVID J. DAVIS, one of our best friends, and one of the oldest citizens of Macon. He expired at his residence in this city, on Friday last...MR. DAVIS, for the last ten years, had been alternately Sheriff and Deputy Sheriff of Bibb county, and held the latter position up to the period of his last illness. He will long be held in the affectionate remembrance of this community.

Married – On Friday, 16th inst., by LEWIS LINCH, Esq., MR. JOHN R. SHOCKLEY, of Upson county and MISS CATHERINE JENNINGS of Putnam county, Ga.

Died – At Hudson, N.Y. on the 17th inst., of dropsy of the brain, EDITH MANNUS, infant daughter of WM. C. and CAROLINE H. B. RICHARDS, of New York, aged 13 months.

On the 30th a marriage took place on a cake of floating ice in the Ohio river, opposite Rising Sun, Indiana, when the Rev. MR. COLLARD united the Rev. JAMES H. BROOKING to MISS SALLIE CRAIG, all of Boone county, Kentucky.

GEORGE W. GREEN, the wealthy banker, who was convicted some time since of the murder of his wife (?) hung himself in his cell at Chicago, on Sunday morning last.

Issue of March 6, 1855

It is said that a Dagurreotype of GREEN, the wife poisoner, who committed suicide in Chicago Jail, was taken while he hung suspended and lifeless from the beam. Great curiosity is expressed to see it and innumerable copies are being made.

JOHN TABOR, who is to be hanged at Stockton, California, for the murder of JOS. MAUSFIELD, was formerly editor of the Stockton Journal and one of the best newspaper writers in California.

A bootmaker, named BENNETT, was severely but not dangerously stabbed in the abdomen on the 27thult., in Americus, by MR. JOHN WESTBROOK.

Issue of March 13, 1855

Married – On Monday evening, March 5th, at the Methodist Episcopal Church, by the Rev. MR. HINTON, MR.

WILLIAM H. BRAY to MISS MARY B. SIMS, both of this city.

A German family in New York were recently poisoned by eating raw bacon ham. Two of them, WM. WISE and wife, are dead, and the third person, also an adult, is not expected to recover.

Judge EDWARDS, of the Supreme Court of New York, died Tuesday last. He was a grandson of the Rev. JONATHAN EDWARDS, author of the celebrated "Treatise on the Will".

Issue of March 27, 1855

Married – On Tuesday, 6th instant, at the residence of MRS. J. MITCHELL, by M.MANNING, Esq. MR. WARREN D. WOODS, of Macon, and MISS SARAH A.P. MITCHELL, of Hawkinsville.

Issue of April 10, 1855

Charge of Murder on the High Seas – The Baltimore Patriot of Friday evening contains the following paragraph Captain HENRY C. BURCH, master of the schooner Susan Cannon, was arrested yesterday by Marshal WATKINS, on the charge of causing the death of JAMES BAKER, a colored seaman of the schooner, on the voyage from Baltimore to Charleston, S.S. and back. The Susan Cannon is a regular packet between the two ports, and it is charged that on the voyage hence to Charleston (the schooner sailing on the 22d of February) the captain beat BAKER with a belaying pin and stick of oak wood in the most severe manner, so that the blood came out of his nose and ears. On the 16th of March, on the return voyage BAKER died, about four o'clock in the morning, from the injuries alleged to have been received at the hands of the Captain. One of the crew testifies that on voyage home, as additional punishment to BAKER, the Captain had buckets of cold salt water thrown over him. BAKER was about 30 years of age, and has a father and mother, he stated, living on Fell's Point. His body was buried at sea. Capt. BURCH was committed in default of the sum of $5,000 for his appearance at a further examination before JOHN HANAN Esq. U.S., Commissioner.

Issue of April 17, 1855

The death of MRS. CASS, the wife of the American Minister at Rome, has been already mentioned. It is stated that she died from congestion of the brain, caused by taking a hot bath, too soon after eating. She was seized in the bath, and lived but an hour, unconscious. It was in May last that she was married to MR. C. at Paris, and she is said to have been a young lady remarkable for her accomplishments and personal attraction.

Death of BENJAMIN E. STILES, Esq. – It is with deep regret, that we announce to our readers the death of BENJAMIN E. STILES, Esq., who breathed his last in Savannah on Tuesday, the 10th inst. For several years, a resident of Vineville near this place, MR. STILES was well known to most of our citizens, by whom he was highly esteemed and respected. He was an upright and honorable man, a public spirited citizen, an honest politician, and a cultivated gentleman. He will long be held in the friendly remembrance of this community.

Died – In this city on Monday evening, 9th instant, MR. WILLIAM T. MIX, in the 35th year of his age. MR. MIX was a native of Connecticut, but had resided in this city for the last six years...

On Tuesday morning, 10th instant, MR. JOHN DACY, in the 45th year of his age. MR. D. has left a wife and four children to mourn his death.

In Savannah, on Tuesday the 10th of April, BENJ. E. STILES, in his 61st year.

Issue of April 24, 1855

Homicide – About noon yesterday a difficulty occurred in the vicinity of the drinking saloon adjoining the Holland House between MR. DANIEL DOUGHERTY and JAMES MARTIN, which resulted in the death of MR. DOUGHERTY by a stab from a knife in the hands of MARTIN. He survived but a few minutes after receiving the wound. MARTIN was at once arrested and lodged in jail. In regard to the particulars of the affair we have heard several conflicting statements, but as MARTIN will probably receive his trial this week, (the Superior Court being now in session in this city) we defer any further account of the matter for the present. MR. DOUGHERTY was one of our old and valued citizens and his loss will be regretted by a large circle of friends and acquaintances. Atlanta Intelligncer, April 18.

Issue of May 1, 1855

Homicide in Charleston – An affray occurred on Friday night last, on board the schooner William and John, lying at POTTER's wharf, on which a man by the name of BARNEY MCGUIRE was killed by a stab through the heart. An inquest rendered a verdict of murder against MICHAEL and JAME CONOWAY, brothers, one of whom was attached to the schooner as a seaman. They have been committed for trial, and two others named QUINN and NOLAN have also been committed upon suspicion of being implicated in the affair.
Charleston Mercury

Married – In this city, on Wednesday evening, the 18th instant, by the Rev. C. D. MALLARY, MR. E.A. ROBERTS to MISS EMMA N. HINES, all of this city.

Died – In Baker county, on the 18th inst., of consumption, MRS. DOLLY COLQUITTE, wife of Hon. A. H. COLQUITT, and daughter of the late Gen. H. H. TARVER, of Twiggs county. Her body was brought to this city, and interred in Rose Hill Cemetery on the 20th inst.

In the city of Savannah, on the morning of the 26th of April, ANN MARIA, daughter of J. JOSEPH and JULIA ANN HODGES, aged 6 years and 24 days.

Issue of May 8, 1855

Death of WALTER T. COLQUITT – It is with deep regret that we announce the demise of the Hon. WALTER T. COLQUITT, one of the most brilliant and gifted of the citizens of Georgia. He died yesterday at the house of WM. ROSE, Esq. in this city, after a long and painful illness...

Robbery of a Georgian – The New York Herald of Saturday says: SILAS SMITH was arrested in Rogers' Hotel in Fulton street by Sergeant STOUGHTON and Officer SHANGLE, of the reserved corps, charged with being implicated in a high-way robbery that took place in the Second Ward about a week ago, wherein a gentleman named JAMES MCGLINSEY, a resident of Augusta, Ga. was knocked down and robbed of $85. The complainant states in his affidavit that when he arrived in this city in the steamship Southerner, from Charleston, he was met by SMITH with whom he took sundry drinks at various saloons in the neighborhood of Park Row. Wishing to inquire the way to the residence of a brother of his, who lived in Fifteenth street, he requested SMITH to show him the way. The request was readily granted, and while in company with his new-made acquaintance, he avers that he was knocked down and robbed of the above amount. The accused, who is quite a respectable looking personage, was found lying very ill at the hotel before mentioned, from a sore leg, and was so badly injured that his conveyance to the Tombs in a carriage was deemed necessary. The magistrate committed the accused for examination.

Fatal Effect of Lightning – During a thunderstorm at Arkadia, Madison county, Missouri, on the 17th inst., the lightning struck the Arcadia High School building, which took fire and burnt, consuming four of the pupils. One of the boys was HARRY, son of F. L. RIDGELY of St. Louis.

Married – At the residence of MARTIN BURNETT, in Knoxville, Ga., on the 3d instant, by C. H. WALKER, J.P. NATHAN CHILDRE, JR. to MISS ELEANOR ELIZABETH WHITAKER.

At the house of NATHAN CHILDRE, SR. in Crawford county, Ga., on the 29th inst., by C.H. WALKER, J.P., HENRY Y. REVELL to MISS MARTHA CHILDRE.

Died – At the residence of his son, NATHAN C. MUNROE, in Vineville, on the 24th ultimo, NATHAN C. MUNROE, at the advance age of eighty-two years. MR. MUNROE was a native of the Sate of New York where he was a merchant for many years.

Issue of May 29, 1855

Melancholy Event – MRS. BLACQUE, daughter of DR. MOTT, New York, and wife of the interpreter to the Turkish legation here, has just died suddenly. The cause was the reception of a letter from her husband, stating that he had married another wife – a Greek lady – as it was his clear right to do according to his religion and the customs of his country. He added that he had no desire ever to see her again.   Paris Cor. New York Times

Death of MRS. DR. BLAQUE in Paris – In contradiction of the false and cruel assertion of the Paris correspondent of the Daily Times of the 19th inst. in reference to the severe bereavement to my family in the death of my daughter, MRS. BLACQUE, in Paris, of typhus fever, I hasten to publish a paragraph from a letter just received from her physician and my friend, DR. BERTIN.
It is in order to do justice to the absent that I feel constrained to make this publication.
In allusion to certain uncharitable rumors which had been circulated in Paris, he says: I was at first induced to attribute the violent symptoms in your dear daughter's case to the moral effect of a letter received from Constantinople. Like most Americans here, I myself was greatly prejudiced; but I have since then examined the letter referred to which, with all others, is now in the hands of the Duchess de Valmy. My conscience constrains me to say that I find nothing in it whatever which in any way could have produced the effect attributed to it. Paris May 3, 1855 VALENTINE MOTT.

Died – In Jones county, on the 17th inst., MRS. HELEN M. ROBERTS, wife of MR. A. ROBERTS, and sister of MR. TW. BRANTLEY of this city, in her 22nd year.

On the 23d inst., at his residence in this county, JOSEPH CARR, in the 77th year of his age. He was a native of North Carolina, but for the last sixty years resided in this State.

Issue of June 12, 1855

Two brothers named LANDERMANN, employed on a canal boat, lost their lives on the night of the 20th, at Maunch Church, by suffocation from coal gas.

Issue of June 19, 1855

A Gallows Speech – JAMES PARKS, who on Friday last was executed at Cleveland, Ohio, made quite a long speech before his execution, asserting his innocence. The following reference to his family was made: I leave a dear wife, who has, in my long confinement been an angel in her solitude and care for me. I had never know her virtues, had it not been for my misfortunes. I leave a dear infant who has been taught to clasp its arms around my neck, and whom I love dearly. I leave aged parents, now near eighty years old from whose kind hearts I had hoped to keep the ignominious fate of their son: (Here his voice faltered, and he burst into tears). It was for the sake of all these that I attempted yesterday to shorten my life a day. When I am taken hence give my body to my wife. I commend her and the child to you. Let her not suffer in wont. Here some kind person proposed to express the feelings of those present by taking up a contribution, and it was done on the spot: $44.60 was contributed. On seeing it, PARKS seemed moved by the kindness, and thanked them with considerable emotion. He concluded by declaring his innocence and gave the signal for his execution, by dropping a handkerchief.

Died – On the 2nd inst., MRS. MARIA FOSSIM OSBORNE, wife of JOHN H. OSBORNE, of this city. MRS. OSBORNE, was a native of Charleston, S.C. but had resided for many years in this State, at St. Mary's and at this city.

In Marietta on the 9th inst., ELLA CALEDOCIA, youngest daughter of the Hon. C. J. MCDONALD.

Issue of June 26, 1855

Died – At the residence of DR. J. C. HARNEY, near Knoxville, Crawford county on the second day of June, DR. RICHARD HARVEY, in the fifty-eighth year of his age.

The deceased was a native of Hancock county but removed to Crawford county soon after its settlement, where he continued to reside up to the time of his death...

In Roswell, Georgia, on the morning of the 19th of June, ELIZABETH M. infant daughter of MR. and MRS. PROUDFOOT, aged 2 years and 7 months.

Died, on the 22nd inst, CARRIE ALIDA, daughter of A.A. and C. E. MENARD. Aged 13 months and 5 days.

Issue of July 3, 1855

Our readers will remember the case of NED DAVIS, a negro man belonging to MR. JAMES DEAN of Macon, who sought to escape to the North in March, last year, on board the steamship Keystone State. He had concealed himself beneath the guards of the steamer but was discovered before her arrival at Philadelphia, and lodged in jail in Newcastle, Delaware. After a full investigation of the case, he was remanded to his owner, who sent him to his plantation in Southwestern Georgia. We now learn that NED DAVIS has made a second attempt to escape. It is said, he succeeded in fastening himself under one of the cars of the night passenger train, which left Macon the evening of the 11th inst. for Savannah. He had dressed himself in a new suit of broad cloth and over this had put his ordinary clothing for protection, intending when he reached Savannah to cast off the latter. On the arrival of the cars at Millen, some one passed along the train with a lantern, when it was observed by the conductor that the bottom of one of the cars cast an unusual shadow and upon examination it was found to proceed from NED and his perch beneath the train. He was at once secured and returned to his owner. Had he succeeded in getting to Savannah, he would doubtless have made another effort to reach the Northern States.

MR. WILLIAM LEWIS of Taylor county, committed suicide by shooting himself with a pistol on the 24 inst. It is said that domestic misunderstanding was the moving cause of the fatal act. The deceased was 53 years of age.

Issue of July 10, 1855

Married – On Sunday morning, 24th ult., by C. H. WALKER, Esq., JONATHAN COLBERT to MRS. NANCY HARRIS, all of Crawford co., Ga.

Died – At Indian Springs, Ga., of Dropsy, on the 3d of July, WILLIAM KING, in the 39th year of his age. He was a native of the State of New York, but for sixteen years a resident of this city...

Issue of July 17, 1855

Death of an Ex-Member of Congress. The Lynchburg Virginian mentions a rumor that DR. AVERETT, of Halifax, Va., formerly a member of Congress, went to his study, a few days ago, with a lighted cigar and laid down on a lounge, when probably falling to sleep, his cigar set fire to a thickly wadded dressing gown, which he had on. He was soon covered in flames, and either from suffocation of the inhaling of flame, expired.

RICE and DRISCOLL, the Lafayette, Ind. Murderers, have been sentenced to be hung on Friday, the 14th of September.

MR. DAVID BURTON, who was shot near Smyrna, Del. A few weeks ago by a negro man, TOM OLIVER, died on Wednesday last. Distressing circumstances are connected with the case. The wife of MR. B. was sick at the time of his being shot; upon hearing of the occurrence she became very feeble and died in a few days after, leaving a young child in delicate health, which soon followed its mother in the train of death.

MR. WALTERS, overseer of MRS. FLINT, near Alexandria, Louisiana, was cruelly murdered on the 8th inst. Twelve negroes were arrested.

A negro was arrested by the citizens of Navidad, Texas, for distributing poison, among the slaves along the river. He was liberated by his master, a man named WHITE and secreted. Great indignation was felt, and if caught, the punishment of the Negro will, no doubt _____.

DAVID ORNDOFF, who was shot a short time since in Hampshire county, Va., by S. MCDONALD, has since died of his wounds.

Issue of July 24, 1855

MRS. CATHERINE SCHOLEY, the largest woman in the world, died in Sciota township, Piquo county, Ohio, while sitting in her chair, on the 5th inst.

Married – At Tranquilla, Jones county, on the 12th inst. by the Hon. JOSEPH DAY, DR. GEORGE W. FARRAR, of Jasper county, to MISS FANNIE J. E., daughter of R. B. DAY, of Augusta.

In Jones county, on the 15th inst. by JAMES T. RENFROE, Esq., MR. WILLIAM A. HARTHON of Monroe county, to MISS SARAH DAVIS of the former place.

Issue of July31, 1855

Died – Near Macon, on the morning of the 24th inst., THOMAS CLARENCE, son of JAMES N. and SARAH ANN KING, aged 27 months and 11 days.

Issue of August 7, 1855

On the 16th inst. a man named DAVID STODDARD was executed according to legal sentence, at the Rock Island, Illinois jail, in presence of the military and a large concourse of persons, for the murder of his wife. On the scaffold he confessed his crime, and charged it to habitual intemperance.

The Columbia Times records the death, at Winnsboro of DR. J. C. CALHOUN, son of the great statesman; also, of cholera, at Sebastopol, DR. JOHN MCMILLAN, a son of JOHN R. MCMILLAN, Esq. of Aberdeen, Miss., formerly of Columbia. He reached Sebastopol on the 1st May, full of ardor and enthusiasm in his profession, which in one short month were cut short by the terrible disease now prevailing in the Crimea.

Murder of MR. A. J. ORR. Our readers have doubtless already heard of this terrible catastrophe through other channels. MR. ORR was murdered by one of his own negroes – a runaway whom he had reclaimed from a Carolina jail, and was taking him back to his works on the Gulf Road, a few miles from Savannah, at the time when he was killed. The murderer was arrested on Thursday at a country store, on the Hinesville road, and was taken at once to Savannah, where he is now lodged in jail. MR. ORR was a resident of this place and leaves a family and many friends in this vicinity, who have been plunged into the deepest grief by this terrible event.

One of the Cincinnati papers published a rumor that an affray had occurred at Dripping Springs, Ky., on Saturday week, in which DAVID S. GOODLOE and CLAY SMITH were killed and CASSIUS M. CLAY dangerously wounded. The rumor prevailed at Lexington, Ky., whence it was telegraphed, but another dispatch contradicted it, on the strength of a letter from Richmond, Kentucky which says that no ____ took place at Dripping Springs on that day.

Married – On Sunday evening, July 29, at the Catholic church, by the Rev. DR. O'NEIL, M. V. BARRY, Esq. to MISS CATE LEONARD, all of this city.

Died – In Jones county, on the 28th ult. WM. E. M. DRAWHORN, of Dooly county, in the 19th year of his age.

$30 Reward – Ranaway from the subscriber on the 20th inst., a yellow boy named RUFUS, between 17 and 18 years of age, has thick lips, pleasant in disposition and manners, and weighs between 130 & 140 pounds. Also, a mulatto woman named MARGARET, but calls herself MARGARET GREEN, about 23 or 24 years of age, and weighs about 130 pounds, she was born in Laurens county, and raised in the BLACKSHEAR family from which I purchased her. She was well dressed, had on a bundle of good clothing, and I believe she is now making her way to Columbus, and will no doubt pass for white, having but one-eighth negro blood in her, she having decoyed the boy off, will in all probability pass him off as her property. A reward of $10 will be paid for the woman and twenty dollars for the boy, if taken and lodged in any Jail so that I get them. The boy is a fine and intelligent boy, and well known about Macon. My address is Francisville, Crawford county, Ga.

R. B. SMILEY

Issue of August 14, 1855

Sentenced – JOHN T. BOYD convicted as accessory with DAVID WRIGHT, in the murder of ALEXANDER M. ROBINSON, deputy Sheriff of this county; and WILLIAM, the property of PITTS & HATCHER were, to-day, sentenced to be hanged on Friday, the 7th day of September

next between the hours of 10 o'clock A.M. and 2 o'clock P.M. When the question was asked by the Court if he had any reasons to offer why the sentence of death should not be pronounced upon him, BOYD replied he had, and read to the Court a lengthy paper, in which he protested his innocence, and pronounced the testimony given against him by the witness, ZACH GAMELL, to be false in every particular. At this point, he raised his hand, and called upon God to witness the truth of what he was saying.
Columbus Sun

Desperate Attempt to Escape. Awful Death by Suffocation and Burning. DAVID WRIGHT, who was confined in jail under conviction of murder in the first degree, committed about eighteen months ago, on the person of A. M. ROBINSON, deputy Sheriff of this county, and awaiting the sentence of the Court, which was set for to-day, set fire to his cell on Saturday night last, and burnt himself to death.
Part of the facts elicited before the Coroner Inquest, are these: When found, he had lying near his head, an instrument which resembled both a saw and a knife. It was made of a saw for cutting iron, and is about the size of the large end of a key hole saw, with the back ground sharp and to a point, evidently intended to saw off his irons, and then, if necessary, cut his way through any force that might oppose his escape. When the cuff around his leg was taken off, it was found that he had sawed it nearly two, and it is supposed the heat of the fire, which was built near the spot where he was chained to the floor, became too hot for him to do more, and he was compelled to move his body as far from it as he could stretch himself, in which position he died. Had he succeeded in cutting off the clog, there is no doubt he would have given the alarm of fire, when the door was opened, made an attempt to escape and with the assistance of the aforesaid instruments, might have slayed his third man.

WRIGHT had evidently put himself in trim for getting away. He had stripped off all his clothes but a pair of brown Holland pants, which were buttoned tight around him. With no shirt on, it would have been impossible for any one to hold on to him, and had he relieved himself of the incumbrance, as a shrewed man would have done, before he put the fire underway, he would have had little difficulty in making his escape. However, there seems to have been a destiny about the man. On a former occasion he escaped from jail, and after being gone two months or more, was captured but little over 200 miles from home.
By the exertions of the firemen - who, together with the military, were promptly on the spot – the flames were subdued before the jail building was materially damaged.
Columbus Sun

Death of MR. L. O. REYNOLDS – It is with deep regret that we announce to our readers the death of MR. L. O. REYNOLDS, President of the South Western Railroad Company. A resident of this city, his many excellent qualities both of head and heart had endeared him to a large circle of acquaintances, who are now left to mourn a choice spirit gone, and a genial light extinguished.

Issue of August 21, 1855

Ravages of Yellow Fever – Sad Case. The Richmond Dispatch state that MR. M. B. GODWIN, a compositor in that office, has lost during the prevalence of the epidemic at Gosport, a father, mother, aunt, sister, brother, brother-in-law, nephew, and cousin, all of whom were residents of that place.

MIKE WALSM, who sailed for Europe on Wednesday, is bound for the Crimea, to which place he will go overland through Germany and Russia.

Issue of August 28, 1855

Married – On the 16th inst., by the Rev. CARY COX, D. E. ANDREWS, Esq. of Standfordville, to MRS. MARY M. HOLT, all of Putnam county.

On the 26th inst. by Rev. L. SOLOMON, CHARLES P. REYNOLDS, Esq. to MISS MARY A. E. RHODES all of Twiggs county, Ga.

Issue of September 4, 1855

Married – At Col. WILBURN's near this city, on the 30th August by Rev. S. LANDRUM, MR. WM. C. BANDY of East Macon, to MISS MARTHA M. WILLETT.

Issue of September 11, 1855

MISS DEFORD, a school mistress, at Newburyport Mass., has been fined $10 and costs, about $75 in all, for severely punishing a pupil. She has, however, appealed. Some 500 to 600 ladies, who believed her innocent of the charge, attended the trial.

The trial of the two brothers MASK, who were charged with the murder of MISS SMITH, in Marshal county, Miss., has just terminated at Holy Springs. They were found guilty, and one is sentenced to be hung, the other to fifteen years imprisonment in the penitentiary.
Died, at Macon on Tuesday evening last, NORA, daughter of JNO. B. ROSS, aged 7 years and 6 months.

Issue of September 18, 1855

Died, in this city, on the 27th August, 1855, MRS. ELIZABETH BONE, in the 80th year of her age. She was a member of the Primitive Baptist Church for more than 40 years.

Died, on the 15th inst., at the residence of her son-in-law, MR. C A. ELLS of this city, MRS. SARAH KELSTCH, aged 68, formerly of New Haven, Ct.

Issue of September 25, 1855

An Old Gentleman Charmed Out of Twelve Hundred Dollars – The Gipsies have stolen $1,200 from old MR. PEARSE, of Limerick, Maine. They made him believe that $4,000 was buried in a pot on his farm, and persuaded him to get the $1,200 together and deposit in a small trunk, to remain in his possession six days, while they were working the charm to find out the spot where the $4,000 was hidden. Soon afterward, the Gipsey woman returned, and accused the elderly greenhorn of opening the trunk, thereby defeating "the charm". He considered he had done so, and then the Gipsey woman counted the money again and took the key leaving the trunk and money, as he thought, with MR. PEARSE, but at the expiration of the six days he found that the charm had worked so potently that neither the money not the Gipsies could be found.

Died, in this city, on Friday, the 21st instant, ANN ELIZA LOVE, aged 3 years and 6 months.

In Houston county, Ga., on Thursday, 20th inst. of Congestive Chills, ELIZA. EMELINE, younger daughter of S.S. and ELIZA J. BRYANT, aged 3 years ____ months and 18 days.

Issue of October 1, 1855

Obituary – Article by Montpelier Lodge, No. 104 of Ancient and Accepted Masons for Bro. JOHN H. HOWARD.

A Bloody Tragedy – A correspondent of the Thomasville Enterprise, writing from Telfair county, says a MR. JOHN QUINN eloped with MISS MARTHA WILCOX, daughter of WOODSON WILCOX, of Telfair county, and carried her into Coffee county to the house of MR. JOHN HILL, where they were married by ALEX MOBLEY, A justice of the Inferior Court. After they had been united, the youthful couple started for the house of the bridegroom's father; but while passing a small creek on the road, JOHN QUIN, the bridegroom was shot in the back and instantly killed. His wife went back to the first house, which was MR. JONATHAN ASHLEY's and gave the information that her husband had been killed.
Suspicion rests upon the father of the young lady, and he has given bond for his appearance at the next Superior Court of Telfair.

Execution of a Boy Ten Years Old – The New Orleans Delta publishes the following correspondence from Alexandria, La., recounting the horrid atrocity of the legal murder of a boy only ten years old: The execution of the boy FRANK, for the murder of the Rev. J. J. WEEMS, took place on Friday, the 24th. It is strange, (difficult to read). Some rode forty miles to witness this drama but he was executed and buried by the time they came to Alexandria. On the day before he was called to face death, some gentlemen visited him; but his answers were and could be no other than childish. He was, I believe, only ten years old. The gentlemen told him that the Sheriff was to hang him on the next morning and asked him what he thought of it, and whether he had made his peace with God, and why he did not pray. His answer was – "I have been hung many a time!" He was at the time amusing himself with some marbles he had in his cell. He was playing all the time in jail, never once thinking that death was to claim him as his victim. To show how a child's mind ranges when about to die, I will mention that, when upon the scaffold he begged to be permitted to pray – which was granted – and then he commenced to cry. Oh! What a horrible sight it was!

Served Him Right – A young gentleman, ALONZO GRIFFIN, having expressed sentiments hostile to "the peculiar institution", and given various indications more congenial to the atmosphere of Massachusetts than Georgia, was ordered out of this city on Friday last, and was escorted to the cars on Saturday, by a large company of our citizens. In consequence of his youth and weak head, no violent measures were resorted to, the people only demanding that he should make tracks northbound. We are informed that he stated that there were twenty others of the same sort in Macon and if the statement be true, we hope it will not be long before they are all drummed out of town to the tune of the Rogues March. GRIFFIN is represented to be a crack brained creature, and the proper asylum for all such lunatics is north of Mason's and Dixon's line.

Married – On the 16th ult., at the residence of MR. FIELDS, by the Rev. J. M. FIELDS, F. H. ALLBY to MISS MALINDA WILSON, all of Bibb county.

Died, at her residence, near the city, on the 30th Sept. 1855, MRS. SUSAN F. SHIVERS, in the 57th year of her age, wife of Col. WM. SHIVERS, JR. and second daughter of the late Gov. RABUN. She had long been an acceptable member of the Methodist Church.

In Houston county, at the residence of his mother-in-law, MRS. CHARITY BATEMAN, on the 25th ult. of strangulated hernia, GREEN L. MILLS. He was on a visit, was taken on Saturday night and died on the ____ evening after.

In ____Fla., on the 9th Sept. SALLIE ____ daughter of DAVID and SUSAN BLACKSHEAR.

At the residence of his father in Jones county, on ____, after an illness of but a few days, GEORGE W. WALKER, in the 24th year of his age.

In Houston county on the 9th of Sept., NANCY S., daughter of SEABORN M. and RUTH BATEMAN. (?)

Homicide – We learn that a man named JOHN HASKIE, an engineer on the Georgia Rail Road was murdered in Decatur, on Wednesday night by G. BRICE. HASKIE died of the wound the same night.

A Venerable Couple – MR. JOHN BURROWS, of North Billerica, Mass., is ninety-eight years old, and his wife BRIDGET one hundred! They have lived together seventy-nine years. They are natives of Ireland, and reside with their son VALENTINE BURROWS, at North Billerica. It is doubtful whether there is another couple in America who have been married so long.

Died, of consumption, at the residence of MR. WM. GRAY, MRS. ANNA A. GRAY, wife of JOHN D. GRAY, Esq.

Issue of October 23, 1855

Shocking Murder – Baltimore, October 16. DR. HADELL, formerly of this city, and his brother-in-law C. C. FULTON, Esq. one of the Editors of the Baltimore American, and his student, were murdered by a German, near Cumberland, Md., on Sunday last. Both bodies were stripped and mutilated. DR. HASKELL's head was cut off and buried at a distance from his body.

Judge THOMAS CLINGMAN, was murdered by a slave on the 9th instant, in Carroll county, Missouri. The slave was immediately lynched.

Died, In this city, on the 11th instant, HIBERNIA R., youngest daughter of C. and ADALINE S. MULHOLLAND, in the 10th year of her age.

Issue of October 30, 1855

Wife Murder in Pennsylvania – The Pennsylvania papers contain notice of a supposed murder in Derby, Westmoreland county, Pa. by a farmer by the name of CORRIGAN, on the person of his wife. The accounts say that she was missing for several days, her husband stating that she had gone to Philadelphia when (we copy from a report before us) "On Thursday morning smoke was seen arising from an old quarry on CORRIGAN's premises, some distance from the road, in rather a retired situation, which aroused the horrible suspicion that the woman's body might have been taken there to be consumed, and thus destroy the evidence of her having been murdered. J. O. ATLEK, who resides a short distance from the place, went down to the spot, and found a large fire, made of logs, brush, etc., and omitting a strong smell. On raking among the ashes, he drew out what seemed to be a portion of a human skull. He made the discovery known, and afterwards several other persons went to the fire. They found CORRIGAN working at it. He asked them what they wanted. They told him their suspicions. He said they might search; but again ordered them off and said they were trespassing on his premises. He picked up a stone and threatened to hit one of the persons, who approached, "but the latter also drew a stone, where upon CORRIGAN desisted, and shortly went away. They examined the fire, and obtained more bones.

CORRIGAN was committed for trial on the charge of murder.

The paper from which we have quoted, says, in the conclusion of its statement: There can be no doubt that a most horrible murder has been committed. The woman was probably killed on Saturday night, and her body locked up until Wednesday night or Thursday morning and then taken to the fire and consumed. The circumstances even exceed in atrocity those of the celebrated WEBSTER case at Boston, some years ago. CORRIGAN is well known in this community, and has not borne a good character for many years. He is about 50 or sixty years of age.

Sad Accident – An unfortunate accident occurred on last Thursday evening in the family of our esteemed fellow citizen MR. ABNER JONES. An interesting little daughter, aged some three or four years, had been afflicted with the chills, and with the view of checking them. Quinine had been given, and the night above mentioned, morphine, instead of quinine, was accidentally administered, from the effects of which she died in a few hours.
Selma Sentinel

A German Patriot Gone – On the 14th of September last, JOHN ADAM VON ITZSTEIN, one of the most eminent of the political reformers of Germany, died at his residence, near Hallgarten on the Rhine, aged eighty-one years.

We learn that a duel took place near Fort Pulaski, Savannah, on Saturday last, between JOHN CHAPLIN, Esq., of this State, and DR. KIRK, of Savannah, in which the latter, on the third fire, was killed. MR. CHAPLIN, we understand, fired his first shot in the air, and was slightly wounded in the foot.   Charleston Courier

We regret to learn of the death of WILLIAM POE, Esq. President of the Bank of Montgomery, which took place in the city of Montgomery on Sunday morning 21st instant. He was an estimable and useful citizen, whose absence from the commercial as well as the social circle of that city will be much lamented.   Col. Sun

An accidental Shooting – Yesterday afternoon, in the locality of the Factory, in consequence of some trivial altercation between JAMES ANDERSON and JOSEPH RUDDEL – ANDERSON discharged the contents of a gun at RUDDEL, and a portion of them entered the person of MR. THOMAS LECKIE. The gun shot wounds are not considered dangerous. RUDDEL was uninjured. ANDERSON has been committed to jail. Augusta Const.

Capt. JAMES M'LURE died at his residence, eight miles south east of Chester, in this State, on the 7th inst., in the 70th year of his age. Captain M'LURE was a captain of the State Militia in the war of 1812 with England, and was stationed with a company from Chester, at Charleston and Hadrell's Point.

Married – On the 18th inst. by the Rev. LEWIS SOLOMON, DR. J. T. CHAPPELL of Wilkinson co. to MISS H. A. STANLEY, daughter of IRA STANLEY, Esq. of the county of Laurens.

Died – At his residence in Wilkinson county, of Typhoid Fever, on Saturday the 1st Sept., THADEUS A. THARP, in the 24th year of his age. The deceased was a consistent member of the Baptist church, of which he had been a member from an early age...He had been married about two years...

Issue of November 6, 1855

Afflicting Calamity – We regret to hear that MRS. SALINA STUBBS, wife of MR. SEABORN J. STUBBS of Wilkinson county, came to her death on the 16th inst., in a most distressing manner. The particulars are as follows: MR. STUBBS was preparing to remove to his lower plantation, and while MRS. STUBBS and the servants were engaged in cleaning some furniture, her clothes in contact with the fire, by which she was working, and her dress (calico) at once was in a flame. By the aid of the servants, and MR. BUTLER, who came to her assistance, the fire was extinguished, but not until it had so seriously injured the lady as to ultimately cause her death. Prompt medical attention was had but no good effect, unless a partial alleviation of her sufferings. She died in about 13 hours after the accident.

MRS. S. was 26 years of age, and much esteemed on account of her many good qualities. She leaves two young children and a large connexion, and many friends to mourn her sad and untimely fate.
Fed. Union

Terrible and Fatal Explosion – It is our painful duty to record a most terrible engine explosion on the Central Railroad by which two persons, the engineer, MERRILAND KELLY, a native of Pennsylvania, and first fireman BARNES, from Cincinnati, were instantly killed and the brakeman MICHAEL SHENAHAN, was seriously injured. This sad casualty took place about 2 o'clock Wednesday afternoon, near the 13 mile station, the engine belonging to a freight train coming down. The cause of explosion is not yet satisfactorily explained and probably never will be as the engineer is numbered with the dead. The engine, we understand, was one the Baldwin's make and five years old.

The explosion is described as dreadful in the extreme, the whole Locomotive being thrown forward a distance of nearly fifty, and the track torn up one hundred and fifty feet. The pecuniary damage is estimated at about $7,000. The bodies of the killed were dreadfully mangled.
Sav. Georgian

The Oldest Engineer – NATHIEL CUMMINGS who runs the accomadation train between Waukegan and Chicago, Ill., is said to be the oldest engineer in the United States, having driven the first locomotive placed on a railroad in this country.

Issue of November 13, 1855

The Hon. EDWARD B. DUDLEY, formerly Governor of North Carolina, died at Wilmington on the 30th ult., in the sixty-fifth year of his age.

Died – In Macon, Ga. on the 7th ult., MR. WILLIAM CRICHTON, aged 51 years, a native of Edinborough, Scotland.

In this city, on the 6th inst., ROBERT ATKINSON, only child of A. G. and AURELIA L. BOSTICK, aged 24 months and 6 days.

In Perry, Ga., on the 26th, after a short illness, MR. WILLIAM C. SPEIR, in the 42d year of his age...For years a consistent, devoted member of the M.E. Church.

Issue of November 20, 1855

JOHN WISE, the aeronaut, is of opinion, it is stated, that MR. WINCHESTER, who went up from Norwalk, Ohio, on the 2d instant, was drowned in Lake Erie, as he had not ballast enough to take him over the lake.

Death of a Murderer – The Chambersburg (Pa.) Whig records the death in jail at Huntingdon, of ELIZABETH HARKER, who had lain there under sentence of death since the fall of 1853, for the murder of her husband and afterwards of her sister, by poison. She was 60 years of age, when she was committed the first of these murders.

A negro man, GEORGE, belonging to DR. R. COLLINS, has been convicted of manslaughter for killing a fellow slave, named BRISTER, near Savannah, on the 16th of September.

Married – By CHARLES H. WALKER, J.P. on the 11th inst., ISAAC CHILDRE to DOLASKI JANE DARBY, all of Crawford co., Ga.

In Houston county, on the 14th inst., by the Rev. ROBERT LESTER, MR. JAMES D. LESTER, JR. to MISS BROOKS GUNN.

Issue of November 27, 1855

THOMAS F. MEAGHER, Esq. was on Wednesday married by Archbishop HUGHES, at the Episcopal residence, in New York, to MISS ELIZABETH, daughter of PETER TOWNSEND, Esq. of Orange county, N.Y. MISS TOWNSEND has been one of the reigning belles of the Fifth avenue in New York City.

REUBEN SAMUEL has been convicted in Rockingham county, N.C. of the murder of REUBEN SOUTHARD.

Issue of December 4, 1855

Georgetown, (D.C.) – A distressing occurrence took place yesterday afternoon, by which a lovely little girl-HARRIET, about six years of age, the daughter of MRS. MARTHA and THOMAS CUMBERLAND, was burned to death. The child was playing with lighted paper, the flames of which communicated with her clothing, and before relief could be obtained, her condition was such as to preclude all hope of recovery.

Death of a State Senator – Col. N. H. CLANTON (?) Senator to the Legislature of Alabama from Macon county, died in Montgomery on the 27th inst., of congestive chills.

Death of Hon. P. C. CALDWELL – We note with sorrow the death of Hon. PATRICK CALHOUN CALDWELL. This melancholy event occurred on Thursday, 22d ultimo. On the 2d of October 1852, he had a paralytic stroke, from which he had never fully recovered, and from the effects of which he died. He was born March 10th, 1801, being at his death in the fifty-fourth year of his age.

MR. CALDWELL received his name from the father of JOHN C. CALHOUN, PATRICK CALHOUN, who married his father's sister. He received his academic education from MR. CAMPBELL, at Rice Springs, after which he entered the South Carolina College, where he graduated in December, 1820. After finishing his education, MR. CALDWELL commenced the study of law, and was admitted to the Bar about the year 1822. He proved himself to be a sound and practical lawyer and a good pleader. He was for many years a partner of the late CHAN. CALDWELL. He served with acceptance, the District several terms in the Legislature, and in 1841 was elected and served in the Sessions of the twenty-seventh Congress. The Congressional District was then composed of Fairfield, Newberry and Laurens. At the close of his Congressional career he was elected and served one term in the Sate Senate.   Newberry Mirror

The family of MR. ASAPH WALES (ten in number) is said to have been the only one remaining in Norfolk in which a case of yellow fever did not occur during the lamentable epidemic there.

ROBERT GRAY, aged 93, has just been married, in Fluvanna county, Va., to a lady aged 92 years.

MRS. MARGARET TRUMP, of Massilon, Ohio, states that her husband, G. A. TRUMP, left home Nev. 15, 1854, and has never returned. She wishes any one who can, to turn up that TRUMP, so she can finish out her game of life with him.

PATRICK WELSH, convicted in the Circuit Court of Valparaiso, Indiana, of displacing the track of the Michigan Southern Rail Road, near Bailetown, has been sentenced to ten years imprisonment in the penitentiary – the extent of the law in this case.

Obituary – Died at his residence in Taylor county, on the 31st October, WM. H. LOWE, aged 52 years. He was a member of the Primitive Baptist Church, and had been for many years a Deacon of the same...He has left an affectionate wife and seven children, besides a step-daughter...

Died – In Athens (?), 21st ult. Col. JOHN A. COBB, in the 73d year of his age.

Issue of December 11, 1855

Died – In Oglethorpe, on Wednesday morning the 28th ultimo, aged 26, after a painful illness, MRS. MARY SELMA COLZY, consort of DR. E. F. COLZY of the former place. Death is at all times a painful incident of our nature, but its gloom was heightened in this instance by the victim being the mother of a tender infant not two days old...

Married – On Tuesday morning, the __th inst., by the Rev. ALFRED T. MANN, MR. A. L. WOODWARD to MISS ANTOINETTE HAMMOND, daughter of DR. HAMMOND of this city.

Issue of December 18, 1855

JOSEPH WILLIAMS, convicted of the murder of his father, FRANCIS WILLIAMS, has been sentenced by the Circuit Court of Person county, N. C. to be hanged on the 24th inst. We understand that a petition signed by over

400 persons has been forwarded to the governor of the State praying the pardon of WILLIAMS.

Tracheotomy – A Boston newspaper says: "Yesterday morning, the operation of tracheotomy was successfully performed by DR. A. B. HALL, of this city, upon a child aged between four and five years, to prevent impending suffocation from croup. A silver tube or canula was introduced into the opening of the trachea, and the breathing became immediately relieved, and there are now strong hopes that the child will recover.

KIRKLAND, the street preacher, was found guilty in Cincinnati, last Tuesday, of using "bawdy, lewd and filthy" words during one of his Sunday discourses, and fined $20 – in default of which he was committed.

Married – On the 13th inst., by Rev. S. LANDRUM, MR. T. TISSEREAU, and MRS. AMANDA BURGE, all of this city.

Died – In Oglethorpe, on Wednesday morning the 28th ultimo, aged 26, after a painful illness, MRS. MARY SELMA COLZY, consort of DR. E. F. COLZY.

In this city, on Wednesday morning the 5th inst., at the age of 84, MRS. SARAH NORMAN, relict of the late GEORGE NORMAN of Lincoln county, and Grandmother of MRS. COLZY. MRS. NORMAN was a native of Virginia, but had been for upwards of sixty years a resident of this State.

Died at his residence in Monroe county, Ga., on ____ult. of inflammation of the Brain, ALBERT HARVEY, in the 46thyear of his age...

Issue of December 25, 1855

The POOLE Murder – New York, Dec. 11 – The jury in the case of BAKER, tried for the murder of POOLE, have disagreed and been discharged. They stood 7 for manslaughter, ___ for murder and 8 for acquittal.

Married – At the residence of Judge DAVID OGLETREE, near Forsyth, Dec. 20th, by the Rev. ARMINIUS WRIGHT, MR. PARKER E. JOHNSTON and MRS. MARY M. CROWDER.

Issue of January 1, 1856

Fatal Accident on the S.W. Railroad – The passenger train on the S. W. Railroad last Tuesday night ran over a steer, at Tobesaufkee Creek, and was thrown off the track. The engineer, WM. COLE, was killed outright – the locomotive falling upon and mangling him horribly. A fireman, JAMES HANCOCK, was badly scalded and thrown into the creek, but he was got out and died of his injuries on Thursday. None of the passengers were injured. The track was torn up for the distance of a hundred yards, and the locomotive and cars considerably damaged. MR. COLE, we are sorry to learn, has left a widow and four young children. MR. HANCOCK was a single man.

Another Fatal Accident – A collision took place between the down and up trains on the Columbia Road, near Reynolds, last Saturday morning. Both trains were out of time – one going slowly and keeping a look out, reversed her steam and was in backward motion, as the other struck. A train hand was killed. A passenger, MR. URIAH PAULK, jumped out of the rear car of the backing train, upon the track, was run over, and, it is believed, fatally injured.

Married – In Macon, Ga., Dec. 27th, by Rev. O. L. SMITH, Rev. WILLIAM W. OSLIN and MISS GEORGIA V. HICKMAN.

On the evening of the 25th inst., by the Rev. H. K. _____, MR. LOUIS E. MENARD to MISS MARTHA A. HODGKINS, all of this city.

Funeral Notice – The friends and acquaintances of MR. KILPATRICK and MR. G. P. GLASS, are respectfully invited to attend the funeral of the latter from the Methodist Church this Tuesday afternoon, at 3 o'clock.

Issue of January 8, 1856

Long article on the murder of JUSTUS MATTHEWS.

Death of Hon. JOHN M. BERRIEN. This melancholy event took place in Savannah, at 9 o'clock in the morning of last Tuesday...

Issue of January 15, 1856

Death of D. R. PERRY, Esq. MR. D. R. PERRY, of the firm of D. R. Perry & Co., Waynmanville, Upson county, Ga., died at New Bedford, Mass. On the 21st December last. He was a pioneer in the cotton manufacturing business of Georgia, being a prime mover in the establishment of the first Georgia cotton mill.

Married – On the evening of the 8th inst., at the house of JAMES VASAGE in Crawford county, Ga., by C. H. WALKER, J.P., THOMAS NELSON WILLIAMS to SARAH CAROLINE WILLIAMS.

In Vineville, at the residence of P. SOLOMON, Esq., on Wednesday evening the 9th inst., by the Rev. H. R. REES, MR. EMMET R. JOHNSON to MISS GERALDINE GRIFFIN, daughter of the late LARKIN GRIFFIN, Esq.

Issue of January 22, 1856

Homicide in Harris county – On the first day of the current month, JOSEPH BUCHANAN killed JOSEPH GORHAM in a fight at Hattack's Grocery in Hamilton.

FANNY FERN Married Again – The New York papers announce the marriage on Saturday last of the far-famed FANNY FERN, MRS. SARAH PAYSON ELDRIDGE, to MR. JAMES PARTON of that city, and author of the "Life of Horace Greeley".

Married – On the 15th inst. by Rev. A. M. THIGPEN, MR. ROBERT H. BARRON, of Clinton, to MISS ELLEN A., daughter of MR. DAVID P. BROWN of Baldwin county, Ga.

The Death of BIG HARPE – About seven miles from Hopkinsville, Ky., at the fork of the road, formerly stood an old and thunder-riven oak, known, twenty years ago, as the "Lonesome Post Oak". In the early settlement of that county – half a century ago – it was the only large tree to be seen for miles around, and hence its name. It became the monument of one of the most desperate single-hand combats known in the prolific history of the border adventure. Near it the heroic DAVIS slew BIG HARPE.
The BROTHERS HARPE – contradistinctively called BIG and LITTLE – were the terror of that (then) thinly settled region of country. Two more execrable monsters never disgraced humanity. They lived with two women as bad as themselves, in a cave, about twenty miles from the tree. Blood and massacre was their delight; they murdered without the ordinary incentives. It was their custom to sally forth and murder, without distinction of age or sex, whomever an object or a whim designated as a victim. As that rich and fertile country gradually settled up, the people determined no longer to submit to their depredations. Some fresh outrage prompted a simultaneous movement - men and dogs collected and took the track.

They came to the two HARPES in a narrow valley, about two miles from the tree. They immediately remounted their horses and dashed off towards their cave. They soon separated, in order to divide their pursuers and improve their chance of escape. Both were mounted on good horses. The pursuit naturally divided, the major portion, however, taking the track of BIG HARPE.

DAVIS, who was mounted on a splendid horse, not only led the pursuit for BIG HARPE, but left his friends far behind. About two miles beyond the Lonesome Post Oak he came up with his antagonist.

Here were two powerful men, armed with rifles, butcher knives and tomahawks, alone, far from help, and bent on death. DAVIS well knew that if overpowered, he would certainly be killed; and HARPE had determined to die rather than be taken alive. They passed and repassed each other, frequently making blows without effect, each dreading to fire for fear of missing, and thereby placing himself at the mercy of his adversary. Finally, the horse of BIG HARPE fell and threw his rider, then rose and galloped off. HARPE instantly sprang to his feet and fired at DAVIS' horse, which reared and fell. They were now no more than ten yards apart. HARPE, whose sagacity was equal to his ferocious courage and villainy, kept dodging and springing from side to side approaching DAVIS, however, by imperceptible degrees. DAVIS, discovering that he would soon lose the benefit of his rifle, fired, but without effect. Each man now drew his knife, and they closed in mortal combat. Very soon they fell side by side, but at this juncture, a large wolf dog belonging to DAVIS, came to his master's assistance, and seized HARPE by the throat. This produced a division in favor of DAVIS, who immediately recovered himself and stabbed his opponent to the heart.

DAVIS's friends soon came up, and removed the body to the Lonesome Post Oak, at whose roots it received coffinless burial.

LITTLE HARPE escaped, went down to the Mississippi and joined the band of the notorious MASON on Stack Island. Soon after HARPE joined him, MASON attacked a flatboat at Cincinnati, and killed all the hands. In consequence a large reward was offered for MASON – to obtain which LITTLE HARPE cut off his head and carried it to Natchez. But here he was recognized as the murderer of MR. WINTERS, was arrested, tried at Greenville, Miss. and executed.

Issue of January 29, 1856

MISS JOSEPHINE LOUISA LEE, of New York, was married recently at the American Legation in Paris, to the BARON DE WAECHTER, Minister of Wortemburg to France.

A man named THOMAS, aged 75 years, reputed to be wealthy and of high social position in Washington county, Pa., has been convicted at Pittsburgh, of forging a promissory not for $465.

Execution of Three Murderers – We find the La Fayette (Ind.) Courier of January 11, an account of the execution of the murderers, RICE, DRISKILL and STOCKING. The courier says: At ten minutes past two o'clock, this day STOCKING, RICE and DRISKILL were duly executed by the hands of the sheriff, THOMAS JEFFERSON CHISSOM – the first named for the murder of JOHN ROSE, and the two latter for the murder of CEPHAS FAHRENBAUGH.
At 12 o'clock they were asked if they were ready for dinner. RICE replied, "Yes, I am hungry." DRISKILL said that he wanted "a good old dinner, as it was the last; he didn't want to die hungry." He remarked to RICE, "we'll get supper somewhere else, ABE." The dinners were brought in and dispatched with great heartiness. After dinner, each of them in turn washed and dressed himself for the

final moment. They could not have made their toilet with more deliberation and coolness if they had been going to a frolic. DRISKILL, when washing, remarked through the window, near which he was standing, to some one outside, that he was "getting a good ready." In putting on his shirt, RICE discovered that there was a button missing. DRISKILL told him to sew one on. RICE replied that he hadn't time. DRISKILL nonchalantly rejoined that there was "an hour yet". He complimented RICE with looking "d__d starchy." RICE, as he finished, observed, "Well, gentlemen, I reckon there was never a willinger soul to die than I am." STOCKING said nothing, but conducted himself (as he did throughout) with great dignity and firmness.

The sheriff then proceeded to adjust the fatal ropes. RICE requested that a stool which had been placed for his accommodation on the scaffold might be removed, and on his request not being immediately complied with, he removed it himself. He then knelt down, inclined his head forward, remarking that he had "seen men hung", by which we understood he regarded that as the proper position. DRISKILL, on observing it, said, "ABE, are going to kneel?" RICE answered, "Yes". He then turned to STOCKING and said, 'STOCK, which way is the easiest to die – kneel or stand? I want to die the easiest way." STOCKING replied that he should stand unless he thought there was danger of the rope breaking. The sheriff assured him there was no danger. He therefore stood up, but DRISKILL kneeled. The caps were then drawn over their faces. And at twenty-two and a half minutes after two o'clock the bolt was withdrawn and the culprits launched into eternity.

Married – On the 22nd inst., by the Rev. J. BASSETT, MISS CHARLOTTE F., daughter of JAMES GUERY, of Houston, to FRANK P. GAREY, of Macon.

Issue of February 5, 1856

A Monster Criminal – The English papers record the arrest of a man named EVANS on a charge of having poisoned his wife, his brother, his friend and thirteen other persons. His wife, before marriage, was a ward in Chancery and entitled to a large fortune. Her guardian resolutely opposed the match, and the Master in Chancery also withheld his consent for some time. Both finally yielded to the entreaties of the young lady, and yet it is believed that she was subsequently murdered by her infamous husband. He was a finished gambler, and a master spirit of the turf, and his friend, MR. JOHN P. COOK, gave him his fullest confidence, and yet suffered the same awful fate. In the case of his brother, MR. WALTER PALMER, insurance on this life were effected to the extent of 23,450 pounds, and then he also, as is believed, was poisoned. Nay, it is stated, that the names of no fewer than sixteen are mentioned as having suffered death by poison, through the agency of the prisoner.

We regret to learn, by a telegraphic dispatch received in this city, the death of ANDREW J. MILLER, Esq. He died at his residence in Augusta. MR. M. was a Senator from Richmond county in the present Legislature.

Arrest in Columbus – JOHN CHISOLM, a young man under twenty and occasionally employed in the Columbus Post Office, was arrested in that city for purloining money from the Post Office last Monday.

Issue of February 12, 1856

Death in a Ball Room – We learn that a melancholy affair occurred on Thursday, the 3d instant at 'Greene's Bottom, in St. Charles county, in this State. MRS. MALINDA TAGGART, daughter of SQUIRE GREEN, while in the midst of an assembly of ladies and gentlemen, engaged in a social promenade, exhibited some signs of indisposition, and requested a sister of hers to take her place in the set in which she was engaged, while she warmed herself. She immediately went to a settee near the stove, and sat down, while the company observing nothing extraordinary in her actions, continued on in their innocent amusement. A few minutes after one of the company, on approaching her, found, to her indescribable horror the young lady a corpse! She was thought to be in good health, and we have heard no reason assigned as to the cause of her death.   St. Louis News

MR. JOHN MAGRATH, an old merchant of Charleston, died Wednesday morning.

Died – In this city, on the 2d inst, after a few hours illness, MRS. EMMA GREEN, wife of MR. J. W. GREEN, in the 19th year of her age, daughter of MRS. BOYLE, of Jones county.

On the 6th inst., at the residence of his Mother, near this city, DAVID F. RILEY, in the 21st year of his age.

On the 29th ult., of Pneumonia, at the residence of JOHN M. ROBERTSON, Fairchild District, S. C. MRS. LAURA ELLEN, wife of NATHAN C. ROBERTSON, and daughter of ISAAC WINSHIP, of Atlanta, Ga.

Issue of February 19, 1856

The Slave Case at Cincinnati – The grand jury at Cincinnati have found a true bill for murder against PEGGY, as principal, and the rest of the adult Kentucky fugitive slaves as accessories, to the murder of the child. The writ was placed in the hands of the sheriff, who when the fugitives were brought to the jail by the marshal for safekeeping, turned the key upon them, and they are now in his possession. No decision has yet been made as to the ownership of the slaves.

Col. ISAAC D'LYON, a well known and highly respected citizen of Savannah died on Saturday last.

Freezing to Death in Florida – JOSHUA J. ARNOW was frozen to death, while crossing Lake George (an expansion of the St. John's river) in East Florida, week before last.

Issue of February 26, 1856

Selling Wives – A short while age ROBERT RHODES was united in the bonds of matrimony with a MISS EASTHAM of Longbridge; but the marriage was unfortunate. Both parties very soon forgot their vows "to love and to cherish" for, shortly after, they relinquished the fascination of each other's charms, and separated. Since this event they have both lived in private lodgings. To bring the marriage knot to a solution, the husband on Monday last, publicly led his wife through the streets of the village in a halter, offering her for sale, when, being viewed by one and examined by another, she was ultimately, after a little haggling, "knocked down" for twenty shillings! The purchaser was GEORGE BANKS, who quietly but ungallantly seized the halter and led her away.

Married – On Sunday, 10th inst., at the house of THOMAS G. SMITH, by C. H. WALKER,J.P. WM. H. VISAGE to MATILDA C. SMITH.

On the 18th inst., at the house of JESSE MORGAN, by C. H. WALKER,J.P., WM. S. KNIGHT to ELIZABETH MORGAN, all of Crawford county, Ga.

In Jones county, on the 6th inst., by G. PETERS, Esq. MR. SOLOMON H. DURHAM, of Gwinnett county to MISS AMANDA R. RITCHIE, of the former place.

In Crawford on the 19th inst., by Rev. R. M. OWEN, MR. DANIEL ROW to MISS MARGARET A. TAYLOR.

Died – On the morning of 9th inst., of Typhoid Fever, at the residence of Col. GEORGE P. SWIFT, at Waymanville, Upson county, SAMUEL G. JEWETT, in the 21st year of his age. He was a native of Springfield, Massachusetts, but had resided at this place for the last six years.

<u>Issue of March 4, 1856</u>

Early yesterday morning a negro woman belonging to MR. JOS. NEWLAND, a merchant and favorably known in this city, decamped from the premises of her master, and by a previous understanding, met a miscreant Abolitionist by the name of ELISHA HYLLER, from New York, on Main Street, as the Portland Railroad Depot, and the twain took passage and repaired to Portland, and thence across to New Albany.
The woman was most gorgeously attired, being dressed in a rich black silk robe, hung with innumerable flounces. A magnificent set of furs graced her shoulders and neck, while over her interesting physiognomy hung a thick green veil. Thus equipped, no one ever suspected her of being of Ethiopian extraction; but the pair were foiled in their endeavor to escape, by a slight indiscretion on the part of the man. After the boat had reached the Indiana side, and when the passengers had gone ashore, the party in question was about to leave also, when the New York gent concluded that he would steal a delectable kiss from her ruby lips; and in order to do this the thick veil was raised, which displayed to the view of the Collector on the boat the color of the woman's face – whereupon he called upon her for her free papers, and they not being forth coming, he instantly brought her back to Kentucky and put her in possession of an officer, who brought her up to the city to the office of ESQUIRE MATLACK, who, after a full

hearing of the case, had her committed to jail to await an order from her master. MR. NEWLAND, up to that period, was not aware that she had left his family residence. At the critical juncture when the woman was seized on the ferry, her valiant and enamored modern New York Don Quixote suddenly disappeared, but vigilant and efficient officers were dispatched in quest of him, who, after a short but diligent search, found him in New Albany, and brought him to this city and lodged him in jail, where he will remain until a speedy course of law shall send him up to Frankfort to serve the State for a few years.   Louisville Democrat

Married – By Rev. R. L. BRECK, on the 21st ult., J. H. ANDREWS, Esq. of South Carolina, to MISS LIZZIE S. DEAN, daughter of Col. JAMES DEAN, of Vineville.

In Crawford county, Ga. on Sunday, 24th inst. by C. H. WALKER, J.P., ZACHARIAH LEWIS to ELIZABETH SANDERS.

In Huntsville, Ala., on the 19th ult., by the Rev. DR. ROSS, EDWARD D. TRACY, Esq. of this city, and MISS ELLEN E. STEELE, daughter of the late Capt. GEORGE STEELE of Huntsville.

Issue of March 11, 1856

A Horrible Death – The Thomasville (Thomas county, Georgia) Enterprise, of the 4th instant, narrates the following: On Thursday last, a few miles from this place, DANIEL KORNEGA, a respectable citizen of this county, was burned to death. MR. KORNEGA was engaged in ginning Sea Island cotton on a roller gin, when he was informed by a servant, in attendance, that the lint was on fire in the room below, where it was received from the gin. He immediately plunged into the lint room through a small aperture, left for unclogging the mouth of the gin, for the purpose of extinguishing the fire, which had not yet caught in flames; but shocking to relate, his entrance into the room produced a current of air which immediately fanned the fire into flame, involving the whole in conflagration.

MR. K. attempted to escape, rushed to the door of the lint room, and called for assistance, but most unfortunately, the door was fastened on the outside with a pad-lock, and the key at that time in MR. K.'s pocket. Thus, doomed to destruction, the unfortunate man resigned himself to his fate; and was taken from the devouring elements, a few hours after, nearly consumed – both arms and legs burned entirely off and only a small portion of his body remained to be interred by his weeping friends.

Birth Extraordinary – The last number of the Herald, published in Camden, Arkansas, contains the following: A few days since a negro woman belonging to Col. JOHN DOCKERY, the worthy president of our railroad, was delivered of four children at one birth – three girls and one boy; their average weight is seven pounds each. When last head from the mother and her little darkies were doing well. The Colonel has named the children after his favorite enterprise – MISSISSIPPI, OUACHITA, and RED RIVER Railroad, giving to the girls the names of the three rivers, and calling the boy RAILROAD. The woman and her husband were both at work upon the Railroad during the past year. This occurrence is regarded as a favorable omen of our road, and it is thought that the stock of the company ought to command a premium and that upon this basis they will be able to negotiate a loan. Hurrah! For the Mississippi, Ouachita and Red River Railroad.

Married – On the 4th inst., in this city, by Rev. S. LANDRUM, MR. DANIEL S. DRIGGARS to MISS ANN M. CLARK.

<u>Issue of March 18, 1856</u>

Accident on the Roanoke and Seaboard Railroad, Weldon, March 11, 1856. The Trestle bridge, twenty miles above this place, gave way, throwing the whole train down 25 feet. Both passenger and baggage cars were burnt up, including baggage and express freight. Killed – Capt. KILKELLY (Express Agent), MR. DAUGHTRY (Mail Agent) CARY and COX news boys. One negro woman is supposed to have been burned entirely up. Capt. BOURDETTE WEYMOUTH, engineer, and three or four others, are badly wounded. J. M. EVERETT and MISS ROWE, of Tennessee, are also injured. There were not many passengers in the train.

Married – In Houston county, Ga., on the 13th inst., by R. J. STORY, Esq., MR. HENRY J. HARVEY and MISS LAURA A. E. WHITE, all of this city.

On the 6th ult., by the Rev. R. A. CONNER, DR. JOHN B. KENDALL, of Upson county, and MISS VIRGINIA W., daughter of JAMES LEONARD, Esq. of Talbotton, Ga.

Obituary – In this city on the morning of the 16th, at the residence of DR. JAS. MERCER GREEN, HARRIET BUEL, only daughter of JAMES R. and F. P. KING, of Roswell, Ga., aged 4 years and 10 days.

Departed this life on the 21st of February, at the residence of DR. AGEE, in Talbot county, MRS. NANCY SLATTER, aged 82 years.

Issue of March 25, 1856

Fatal Disaster – It appears that about half past nine o'clock on Saturday night, the ferry boat New Jersey, of the Philadelphia and Camden Ferry Company, in crossing the Delaware to Camden, took fire in the middle of the stream, and after great difficulty, in consequence of floating ice, was run upon a bar opposite Arch street. There were about one hundred passengers on board, many of whom jumped into the river and were rescued by boats after clinging to floating ice. It is feared that a great number were drowned and burnt. The boat was burnt to the water's edge. Steamers immediately went to assistance of the ferry boat, but the passengers in the water had been previously saved by means of small boats.

Nothing is yet definitely known as to the number who perished. Three bodies only have been recovered, viz: those of JOHN LITTLE, ABRAHAM JANNIE, and FRANCIS FITZPATRICK. Among the missing are SALLIE CARMAN, EDWARD MESCHAMP, formerly conductor on the Amboy Road, an infant daughter of SAMUEL GIVERSON, JOHN FIDELL, MATTHEW MILLER, JR., broker, MR. HOWARD, clerk, MRS. SHADE and child and a large number of colored persons. The origin of the fire is unknown. It burnt out suddenly from the engine room...
Washington Sentinel

Obituary – At the residence of DR. GREENE, in Midway, on the 11th inst. of Bronchitis and Pneumonia, DOCTOR WILLIAM W. HOLMES, Assistant Physician of the State Lunatic Asylum, in the thirty-sixth year of his age.

Married – On Sunday morning, the 16th inst., at the house of JAMES Y. SMITH, in Crawford county, Ga., STEPHEN S. SMITH to MATILDA ANN MILLS.

Issue of April 8, 1856

Good Old Age – MRS. MARTHA THOMAS died at Midway, Georgia, 22d ult. born in Goochland county, Virginia, in the year 1747, and was consequently in her 109th year. She moved to Georgia with her husband several years before the Revolutionary War and settled on the Savannah river, above Augusta, in what was formerly Wilkes, now Lincoln county. They had two sons born before that war was declared.

MR. THOMAS was a brave soldier and was in every hard fought battle in the South. He was at the head of the American column led by La Fayette on the British redoubt at Little York. He was within ten steps of JASPER when he fell at Savannah; was in the battles of Augusta and Charleston, and had two brothers killed at Eutaw.

Married –On Sunday morning, March 30th, at the residence of MRS. MARGARET LOFLEY, near Horse Head, Macon county, by JAMES EDWARDS, J.P., MR. BENJ. F. LEWIS, of Alabama, and MISS ANN ELIZABETH LOFLEY.

Also, at the same time and place, MR. JOSHUA TAYLOR and MISS JANE LOFLEY, all of Macon county.

Died – On 29th of March, SARA LAWTON, infant daughter of JOSIAH A. and ANNE E. FLOURNOY, aged 2 years, 1 month and 18 days.

Obituary – Departed this life, in the sixty-second year of his age, at his residence in Macon county, SOLOMON FUDGE. He was born September 22d, AD1794, died March 28th, 1856. He died as he had lived, a Christian. He joined the Baptist Church AD 1828 and adorned the profession. He joined the order called Primitive Baptist, more properly known, in the opinion of the writer, as the <u>Presbyterian Baptist.</u>

<u>Issue of April 15, 1856</u>

Indian Disturbance in Florida –A small party of Indians attacked DR. JOSEPH A. BRADEN's house, on the Manatee river, in Hillsborough county, on the 31st ult., but were repulsed by a vigorous fire from the house. They carried off seven of the Doctor's servants.

Two privates of the Capt. PRATT's Company U. S. Infantry were killed near Cape Roman on the 30th.

Died – At his residence in Jackson county, on the 19th inst., of Bronchitis and Asthma, HENRY PIKE, in the 53d year of his age.

Remarkable Case – The Rockingham (Va.) Advertiser states that a respectable farmer named SAMUEL HENRY, residing in that county, has totally abstained from food for fifty-seven days! And he may yet survive several days. For some time he has been in a rather melancholy mood, and about two months ago he refused to eat, and since that time has not taken anything except water; and strange to say, he is still alive, though reduced to a mere skeleton. Neither physicians nor friends can induce him to take any nourishment. He declares he can swallow nothing, though he does every now and then take a drink of water.

Issue of April 22, 1856

A Silly Rascal – Somebody signing himself J. V. WILSON, sent to this office for publication three weeks ago, a notice of the marriage of two daughters of MRS. LOFLEY, of Macon county, which were inserted according to request. We now learn that no such marriages took place, and that the letter to us and notice accompanying, were the handiwork of some silly and malicious scamp. We sent both to the relatives of the MISSES LOFLEY, and are glad to learn that the fellow will, in all probability, be identified by the writing and dealt with accordingly.

Death of B. R. GARDNER, Esq. of Milledgeville. The Savannah Morning News, of April 16th, says: "We regret to learn that B. R. GARDNER, Esq. a well known and highly respected citizen of Milledgeville, was killed in Sparta, yesterday morning, by a man by the name of O. J. POWELL. MR. GARDNER, who was formerly a resident of Sparta, was in that town for the purpose of transacting some business in the Inferior Court. A misunderstanding in reference to some pecuniary matter had previously existed between him and POWELL, which is supposed to have been the cause of the killing. MR. G. was shot in the street. Our informant, who left Sparta directly after the melancholy affair, is unable to give us any of the particulars, except that he heard four discharges of a pistol, which, as the deceased was an inoffensive man, who never went armed, he supposes to have been fired by POWELL. He does not know whether POWELL has been arrested.

MR. GARDNER was a wealthy and highly esteemed citizen, and was extensively known in the middle section of the State. He leaves a wife and an interesting family of children.

The friends and acquaintances of MISS SOPHRONIA E. BRANTLEY, JOHN H. BRANTLEY and family, W. S. BRANTLEY, GEO. W. ADAMS and WILLIAM TAYLOR, are requested to attend the funeral of the former at the residence of the latter, this morning at 9 o'clock.

Married – On the 1_the ult. by the Rev. E. W. SPEIR, MISS CARRIE V. daughter of J. B. ROSS (?), Esq. of this city to DR. J. DICKSON SMITH, of Forsyth, Ga.

Issue of April 29, 1856

A Captive Recovered – We find in the San Francisco Herald of March 20, an account of the recovery from the Mohave Indians of a young American girl, about sixteen years of age, named OLIVE OATMAN, whose father and all of her relatives, except a brother and sister, were murdered in the year 1850, about 80 miles from the Gila river. The boy escaped in the darkness, and made known the story of the massacre to a party of emigrants who had found him; but of the two surviving girls nothing had been heard for nearly five years, when, about six months ago, Col. NAUMAN of the U. S. Army, on his way to Fort Yuma, hearing a rumor of there being two female prisoners among the Yuma Indians, caused runners to be sent out, with promises of reward, etc. The elder of the two, the younger having shortly before died, was brought into Fort Yuma, where she was ransomed, and taken in charge by the officers of the post. She was dressed in Indian costume, and had almost forgotten the English language; she was able, however, to tell her name. She bore the marks of severe slavery, and her person was as much developed as that of an ordinary girl of twenty years, especially in the arms, hands and wrists. The Sisters of Mercy of San Francisco had offered to receive the girl into their care

Obituary – Died of Typhoid Fever, at Indianola Texas, on the 2d inst., MRS. ELLEN C., wife of DR. JOSEPH H. BALDRIDGE, in her 22d year.

Died of Consumption, at the house of her brother-in-law, ALPHEUS COLVARD, Esq. in Appling, Columbia county, Ga. MRS. REBECCA J., wife of JOHN THOMAS FULLWOOD, Esq. in her 23d year...Ellen's parting breath was spent in calling for her sister REBECCA; REBECCA unknowing of her sister's death, died repeating her name.

Issue of May 6, 1856

Death of Ex-Governor TROUP – Governor TROUP, according to the Savannah Journal, died at his residence in Laurens county, on the 26th ult. He was born in 1780 and was therefore seventy-six years of age...

MR. JOHN CARNEY, residing on the Alifia river in Florida, was murdered by the Indians, while plowing in his field on the 17th ult.

The distinguished lawyer, OGDEN HOFFMAN, died in New York on the 1st.

Issue of May 13, 1856

Funeral Invitation – The friends and acquaintances of HENRY W. WEED, are requested to attend his funeral at the residence of MRS. E. B. WEED today at 4 o'clock.

Issue of May 27, 1856

The Assault on Sumner – The Constitutionalist of Sunday says: The most reasonable and consequently reliable account of the assault of MR. BROOKS upon MR. SUMNER, states that immediately after the adjournment of Congress on Thursday, while MR. SUMNER was still in the Senate chamber, MR. BROOKS entered and approaching MR. SUMNER, accused him of libeling South Carolina and his grey-headed relative, Senator BUTLER. Immediately after saying which, he struck him with a cane. MR. S. fell to the floor, and MR. BROOKS repeated the caning until MR. SUMNER became deprived of the power of speech. Previously he called for help, but no one interfered until MR. BROOKS had completed his design. MR. SUMNER was then carried to his room.
He was very severely castigated but telegraph dispatches of the following day swore that he would resume his seat in the Senate in a few days. He will be a little more cautious, we presume, how he abuses his Senatorial privileges.
The venom of such a speech as Sumner's could hurt nobody but the author of it. MR. BROOKS adopted the only mode of giving it any sort of consequence or effect other than that of injury to the cause of Black Republicanism.

Assault of Senator SUMNER - Washington, May 22d. MR. BROOKS, Representative from South Carolina, assaulted MR. SUMNER, of Massachusetts, in the Senate Chamber today. SUMNER was seated at his desk, writing, when

BROOKS struck him a stunning blow over the head with a heavy cane, cutting and contusing it badly. The blows were repeated frequently. MR. KEITT, of South Carolina, was present and attempted to prevent any interference. MR. CRITTENDEN, who witnessed the affair, pronounced it a shameful outrage. The provocation is said to be certain remarks used by MR. SUMNER, in his late speech, in regard to Senator BUTLER.

Married – On the 15th inst., by the Rev. JAMES E. EVANS, MR. SAMUEL S. DUNLAP to MISS MARY ANN E. BURGE, all of Macon.

At the residence of J. A. PINTOCK in Marietta, on the 20th inst., by the Rev. T. R. JASPER, Capt. H. J. BARRON, of Clinton, Ga. to MISS OPHELIA D. PINTOCK of the former place.

Died – In this city, on the 19th inst., in the 7th year of his age ALGENON GAILLARD, son of Rev. D. L. and MRS. AMANDA N. SMITH.

In this city, on the 20th inst. WALTER R. son of ALEX. M. and MARY A. SPEER, aged 6 years and 6 months.

At the Madison Springs, on the 15th inst., MRS. MARTHA TYNER, wife of K. TYNER, Esq. MRS. TYNER was for many years a resident of this city...a devoted mother and an indulgent mistress. She was at the time of her death a member of the Presbyterian Church in Macon...Lingering for months in great distress...

In Perry, Houston county, on the 17th inst., GEO S. RILEY, Esq. aged about 27 years.

Issue of June 3, 1856

Digging Their Own Graves – Those men belonging to the command of Col. SCHLESSINGER, who were taken by the Costa Ricans and executed by them were made to perform an unwelcome service just before their exit. Having been condemned to death and their fate announced, the victims were compelled to dig their own graves, and when done, made to kneel upon the margin of the trench dug, when they were shot dead – falling readily into the pit their own hands had dug.

Sad Accident – THOMAS, son of LOTT MALSBY of this city, a lad of ten years old, met with a terrible and in all probability, fatal accident on Sunday afternoon last. While riding on horseback his horse ran away with and threw him, and, foot fast in the stirrup, he was dragged from Ross' Corner to the Female College, a distance of a quarter of a mile, when his foot dislodged. His head was frightfully bruised and fractured and one arm broken. He was still breathing Monday morning.
Since the above was in type, we learn that the lad is dead.

Convicted – Upon another trial before the Bibb Superior Court, THOMAS SORREL was last Saturday found guilty of the murder of the slave SAM, but recommended to the mercy of the Court, by which, we understand, he was sentenced to the Penitentiary for life.

Died – In this city on the 24th inst., MARY, daughter of FREDERICH WM. And CATHARINE M. SIMS, of Savannah, aged 15 months.

In this city on the 17th inst., MISS EMMA IVES, aged 8 years and 6 months; and on the 23dinst., her father MR. EDWIN IVES, aged 42 years – a worthy and much respected citizen. He was a member of the Presbyterian Church in this city...

In this city on the 25th of May, after a few hours illness, SUSAN MARY, only child of WM. B. and ANNA T. JOHNSTON, aged 9 months and 15 days.

Issue of June 10, 1856

Dreadful Affair – The Wilkes Republican of May 30 states that JESSE COCRAHN of Milledgeville, was quarrelling with his son JASPER last week, both being intoxicated, when they attacked each other with knives, and the son fell, stabbed in thirteen places, from the effects of which he died the following day. JESSE COCRAHN was committed to jail, to await his trial in our Superior Court, at September next.

Obituary – Died in this city, after a protracted suffering from Typhoid Dysentery, REBECCA ANN, wife of J. W. BRANTLEY, aged 37 years.

Died – In this city on the morning of the 31st ult., after a protracted illness of 10 months, with slight intermissions, MARY ELIZABETH, second daughter of JAMES H. R. and MRS. MARY ANN WASHINGTON, aged 10 years and 6 months.

Fifty Dollars Reward – Ranaway from the subscriber at Perry, Houston county, Ga., on the seventh day of January last, my negro man MARCUS, about 21 or 22 years of age, 5 feet 10 or 11 inches high, of a light ginger bread color, and round eyes, and when frightened shows the whites very much. He was formerly owned by a MR. GRIFFIN of Columbus, and having kept horses for him on the Stage line, and has relatives in Macon, also at the plantation of MR. WHITTLE in Monroe county. He is well known about Barnesville, Oglethorpe and Americus. I will pay a reward of Fifty Dollars for his arrest and lodgment in any Jail, so that I may get him.

JOHN R. COOK

<u>Issue of June 17, 1856</u>

Died – In this city on the 4th instant, a son of ROBERT BRANTLEY, aged 13 months and 10 days.

Married – At Raysville, Bibb county, on Thursday afternoon, 12th instant, by J. B. ARTOPE, Esq., MR. GEORGE M. CERCOPELY, of Savannah, to MISS HELEN JANE, eldest daughter of J. J. HODGES, Esq. of Bibb county.

On the morning of the 10th inst., by the Rev. G. R. MCCALL, MR. WILLIAM CHAPPELL to MISS MARY MCALLUM, all of Twiggs county, Ga.

<u>Issue of June 24, 1856</u>

Some Nose – The following incident we had from a friend who knew the party: Deacon COMSTOCK, of Hartford, Ct. is well known as being provided with an enormous handle to his countenance, in the shape of a huge nose; in fact it is remarkable for its great length. On a late occasion, when taking up a collection in the church to which the Deacon belongs, as he passed through the congregation every person to whom he presented the bag seemed to be possessed by a sudden and uncontrollable desire to laugh. The Deacon did not know what to make of it. He had often passed around before, but no such effects as these had he ever before, witnessed. The secret, however, leaked out. He had been afflicted, for a day or two, with a sore on his nasal appendage, and had placed a small piece of sticking plaster over it. During the morning of the day in question the plaster had dropped off, and the deacon seeing it, as he supposed on the floor, picked it up and stuck it on again. But, alas, for men who sometimes make great mistakes, he picked up instead one of those pieces of paper which the manufacturers of spool cotton paste on the end of every spool, and which read, "Warranted to hold out 200 pounds." Such a sign on such a nose was enough to upset the gravity of even a puritan congregation.

A Brave Little Fellow – We have a private letter from Wacahoota, East Florida, dated the 12th instant and detailing incidentally the recent assault upon Capt. BRADLEY's house. It was just after dusk in the evening of the 14th May, and BRADLEY lying abed sick. Two of his children – a little boy and girl – were sitting before the open door in the entry of the house, when a band of some twenty Indians stole up and fired upon them. The little girl was killed outright and the boy was mortally wounded; but he nevertheless rose – went in to the family, gave the alarm – took down the gun and fired at the enemy. He then handed it to his brother, saying he had no further use for it, and died immediately. His body had been pierced by two balls. BRADLEY and the other son kept up a fire and the cowardly Indians dare not make an assault. The neighbors finally gathered and drove them off.

Married – Near Hillsboro, on the morning of the 12th June by DR. CORNORELL, WM. A. LANE, Esq. of Clinton to MRS. JOSEPHINE JACKSON of Jasper county.

Issue of July 1, 1856

Death of Gen. T. H. RAYLEY – The well-known member from the Accomac district, we are sorry to see, died at his residence in Virginia last Sunday. No business was done in Congress last Friday after the announcement of this sad event.

MR. BROOKS Indicted – MR. BROOKS has been indicted by the Grand Jury of the District, and his trial was set for yesterday. SUMNER appeared before the Jury as a witness. The House was also to take up the Committee's reports upon the caning affair yesterday.

Died – In Houston county, on Thursday, the 12th instant, JAMES, youngest child of JAMES and MARGARET GUERRY, in the 19th year of his age.

Issue of July 8, 1856

Melancholy Casualty – Last Sunday morning three likely servant lads were drowned in the Ocmulgee, in Macon, while bathing. There were four bathing at the time, and wading hand in hand across the stream, which is low. Three of them got beyond their depth in a hole, and perished before assistance could be rendered them. They belonged to MRS. GEN. SMITH, DR. LIGHTFOOT, and Judge ASA HOLT, and were between the ages of ten and fourteen. Their bodies were all recovered during the day.

Murder – WILLIAM BAKER, of this county, was found dead in a swamp about a mile and a half from town, on Thursday last – his brains beaten out. The story we hear is, that the deceased, in company with others, started out on Monday to hunt runaways – that the party separated for better search and BAKER was heard no more of until found as narrated. The current opinion is that he was murdered by runaways.

Obituary – Died of Typhoid Fever, in Crawford county, on the 27th of June last, after a protracted illness, NATHAN FOWLER, Esq. in the fifty-sixth year of his age. The deceased was a native of Warren county in this State but for twenty-five years past had resided in the county first mentioned...

Died – Near Reynolds, Taylor county, Ga. on Saturday 28th June, after a few days illness, MR. THOMAS T. SHINE – leaving a disconsolate widow and a large family of children to mourn their irreparable loss. MR. SHINE was born in Sampson county, North Carolina, Nov. 24th, 1795, and was consequently near 61 years of age. He had resided in Georgia for the past 17 years...

Shooting of the Mormon Leader, JAMES J. STRANG – Detroit, June 19 – JAMES J. STRANG, the Mormon leader, was shot at Beaver Island, on the 16th, by two of his former followers. He received three balls in the body, and a severe blow from a pistol on the head. STRANG was alive up to noon of the 17th, but he laid in a very critical condition. The assassins had been arrested.

Issue of July15, 1856

Death of Major E. J. HARDIN – The Columbus Sun, of yesterday morning, says: "We regret to announce the sudden death, on yesterday, of Major EDWARD J. HARDIN, an old, well known, and much esteemed citizen of this place. Major HARDIN was born in Warren county, in this State, and in early life, was a merchant in Augusta. He went thence to Florida, and finally removed to this city. He had been at one time Clerk of the Superior Court of Muscogee county, but was not engaged in business at the time of his decease. He leaves a wife and several children.

Married – In this city, on Tuesday the 8th inst., by the Rev. BLAKELY SMITH, MR. HENRY J. KING, of Augusta, Ga. and MISS JOSEPHINE B. FORSYTH of this city.

On the 9th inst., by Rev. SYLVANUS LANDRUM, MR. EDWARD H. GILMER, of Montgomery, Ala., to MISS EVELINA G. LAMAR, of Vineville, Ga.

On the 9th inst., by Rev. S. LANDRUM, MR. CHAS. B. GARWOOD, of Alabama, to MISS MARY KENT, of this city.

Died – At Minerva, Houston county, MRS. CORNELIA A. HAVIS, daughter of JACOB RILEY, Esq. and wife of DR. M. W. HAVIS, aged seventeen years and eight months.

Died, very suddenly, of the highest grade of Billious Fever, involving immoveable-fixed Congestion of the Brain, little JOHN FREDERICK, only son of the Hon. ALFRED H. COLQUITT, of Baker county, Geo; aged three years and nearly six months.

In Houston county, on the morning of the 12th inst., MANORA, the fourth daughter of JOSEPH and CATHERINE E. KEMP, aged twelve months and eighteen days.

Issue of July 22, 1856

Accident on the Central Railroad – On last Wednesday night, the 16th inst., the mail train on the Central Road ran off the track near Robinson's Turn Out, about fifty miles below this city, precipitating the Locomotive from the embankment and badly damaging it. Fortunately, none of the passengers were hurt. The second fireman, ELI WALKER, was killed; the Engineer and first fireman were both injured, but were doing well at last accounts. MR. WALKER was buried on Friday at Fort Valley. The accident was caused, we are told, by the washing up of a culvert by the recent heavy rains in that vicinity. We have not ascertained the damage to the Company.

Fugitive Slave Case – Boston July 17 – WILLIAMS, a fugitive salve from Mobile, secreted on board a vessel, arrived at Boston and was taken before a United States Court and discharged – when the abolitionists hurried him off to Canada.

Shocking Murder of a Young Lady- A letter in the New York Tribune, dated Erie co., Pa., July 8, relates the following tragedy growing out of a love affair: A man by the name of HAYT had for some time been paying his attentions to a MISS ALLEN. He was over 40 years old, while she was in her 15th year. The girl's father had asked HAYT for the loan of a revolver, which he was known to have, to shoot rats with. He had, accordingly, loaded every barrel and after dinner proceeded to the house of ALLEN, for the double purpose of seeing his daughter and delivering his pistol; but after spending some time with the girl she told him that she would not marry him, and that if he was out of the way she could get other beaux or another beau, when without a moment's hesitation he drew from his pocket the pistol, and placing it to her head deliberately fired, when she screamed and fell.

He then picked her up and laid her on the lounge or settee, when he fired a second barrel, the ball passing through her head forward of her ears. The mother of the girl, who was in an adjoining room, on hearing her scream, started to go to her assistance, but HAYT commenced firing at her also, but without effect. He then immediately left the house and ran into the woods, as was supposed for the purpose of secreting himself but instead of so doing, went as quietly as possible and gave himself up to the proper authorities. In his examination he said that he had no intention of shooting or hurting his victim, a minute before the deed was done. He confessed everything, saying he was perfectly sane, but does not know why he fired at the girl's mother, as he did not want to harm her. He was committed.

Issue of July 29, 1856

Fatal Mistake – A Wife Shot By Her Husband – Caroline, July 14th, 1856. Last Friday morning, about 1 o'clock, MR. WILLIAM M. KELLY was suddenly aroused from his sleep, and under the impression that his house was being broken into, seized his gun and instantaneously fired upon some one, as the thought, entering the door; but to his horror he found he had shot his wife, who was fastening it. The shot entered just in front and above the right hip, penetrating deep into the body. Two physicians were immediately called in, but found her beyond hopes. She lingered resignedly and uncomplainingly until about four o'clock Saturday morning, when she died, leaving an almost distracted husband, an infant son eleven months old, and a large number of relations and connections to mourn her loss. MR. and MRS. KELLY had been married nearly two years, and were living most happily together, when the unfortunate occurrence, like a thunder-bolt, destroyed her existence and blighted his. He was, at night, timid, and in the habit of keeping a loaded gun near his bed; hence the terrible accident. Richmond Dispatch

Case of Hon. P. T. HERBERT – Washington, July 22 – The evidence, in the trial of Hon. P. T. HERBERT, for the killing of THOMAS KEATING, has closed. The counsel for the prisoner made a proposition to submit the case without argument, which was objected to by the prosecution.

Strange Sickness in New York – The Herald of Saturday says: A man known as BILLY BARLOW, died at the house 91 Lenord street, yesterday, after an illness of but fifteen minutes. He turned black immediately after his death, and it must be that cholera was the cause. There were several other deaths of the same kind yesterday.

Issue of August 5, 1856

Died – In Perry, Ga., June 30th, J. WESLEY MCEACKIN.

Issue of August 12, 1856

Editorial Affair of Honor – Washington, Aug. 6 – A hostile meeting took place today at noon, near the residence of FRANCIS P. BLAIR, between MR. PRYOR, of the Richmond Enquirer and MR. RIDGWAY, of the Whig, distance ten paces, weapons, pistols. After an exchange of shots, the affair was amicably adjusted, through the intervention of PRESTON S. BROOKS, MR. EDMUNSON and MR. ____ASKIE of the House of Representatives, as mutual friends.

Death of GEORGE T. HOWARD, Esq. – It is our painful duty to announce the death of GEORGE TROUP HOWARD – for the last seven years a resident of Savannah. He had left us a short time since, to visit the home of his family; and about two weeks ago, was taken down with congestive fever. He died, as we have learned, on Friday night, and was buried yesterday afternoon at 3 o'clock. He was the son of Major JOHN H. HOWARD, of Columbus, at which place, we believe, he was born. He was admitted to the bar at McIntosh Superior Court in 1850...

Murder – A murder was committed near this place on Monday the 28th ult., by one DAVID W. GRIFFIN on the body of STANSELL BARBEREE. GRIFFIN struck BARBEREE on the head with a piece of the heart of a board-block producing instant death. The murderer decamped, and has not since been heard of. Bainbridge Argus

Issue of August 19, 1856

Married – In this city on the 18th inst., at the residence of THOMAS W. COLLINS, by the Hon. ABNER P. POWERS, Col. GUSTAVUS FRIEDLANDER to MISS REBECCA R. ROBERTS, both of Brunswick, Ga.

At MR. WOOTON's in this city, on the 14th inst., by Rev. SYLVANUS LANDRUM, MR. JONATHAN D. WINN to MISS EMILY E. BROWN, both of Pulaski county.

Died – In Vineville, on the 7th inst., at the residence of her brother-in-law BURWELL JORDAN, Esq. MRS. E. G. CHAMPION, widow of the late DR. MOSES CHAMPION, of Monticello, Ga.

Issue of August 26, 1856

Death of the Editor of the Courier – We have to record this morning the death of _____ CARROLL one of the editors of the Charleston Courier. He died at about nine o'clock on last evening, after a sickness dating back to but Saturday last. MR. CARROLL was born in Cheltonham, county of Glaucester, England, in 1818 and received his primary education in Somersetshire, where he entered Queen's College, Oxford, in 1837. He came to this country in August, 1849, and in the spring following, became connected with the Charleston Courier, where he has since remained.

Died – Of Congestive Chill, in Albany, Ga. on the 16th inst., ISHAM D. SLEDGE, aged about 45 years, and for the past 20 years has resided in Macon.

Issue of September 2, 1856

Startling News from the West! Louisville, Ky., Aug 26th. A man named PASCHAL D. CRAMDOCK, a notorious character, was mysteriously killed in this city today.

A duel was fought at St. Louis to-day between a man named BROWN and another named REYNOLDS. There was one fire and the former was shot in the knee.

From the Altar to the Grave – A marriage occurred on the 26th of June last in Jefferson county, Florida of MR. THOMAS A. FONDEE, of Sumpter county, Ga. to MISS STATIRA WOOLF. The groom was sick at the time of marriage and died three days after.

Died – In the Warrior District, Bibb county, on the 24th ult., of cancer, ELEANOR, the wife of GEORGE PETTEY (?), aged 62 years five months and 19 days.

In Monroe county LITTLEBERRY LUCAS, of Crawford county, on the 19th (?) inst., after a lingering and painful illness. Deceased had lived to an advanced, being seventy-six years old, he was born in Brunswick, Va., whence he removed to Hancock county, Ga., about the year 1800, where he resided 8 or 9 years, thence he removed to Jones county where he resided until 1823 (?), from there he removed to his late residence in Crawford county where he resided until his death. He left a wife and three children married and settled – besides numerous friends to mourn their loss...

<u>Issue of September 9, 1856</u>

JOSIAH JOHNSON, Esq., Senior Editor of the Fayetteville, North Carolinian, died in Fayetteville, on the 29th ult., of Bilious Fever.

Sad Accident – Yesterday afternoon a sad accident happened off Coxspur Island, which resulted in the death of Lieut. GARDNER...

Married – At the house of SAMUEL W. VISAGE, by C. H. WALKER, on Thursday, 28th ult., JOHN L. WILLIAMS to SARAH JANE MILLS, all of Crawford county, Ga.

On the evening of the 31st August, by JAMES EVINS, Esq., ALFRED MIDDLEBROOKS, Esq., to MISS NANCY C.

WOOTON, daughter of the Rev. JOHN WOOTON, all of Monroe county.

Issue of September 23, 1856

Died – In this city, on the 9th inst. of Billious Cholic, MR. ALEXANDER MCGREGOR, aged about 66 years. He was among the earliest settlers of this city and erected the first framed building west of the Ocmulgee, and the first bridge over the river. Through life, was one of the best and most industrious mechanics of the city.

Obituary – At the residence of her father, MR. JAMES L. HART, in Leon county, Fla., on the 28th inst., MRS. SARAH A., wife of C. EVERETTE JOHNSON, in the 24th year of her age...

Died in Galveston, Texas, on the 2d inst., Col. M. B. MENARD – a pioneer of Texas, and the founder of Galveston City. He was well and favorably known by many in this community...a tender husband, a devoted father...

Issue of October 7, 1856

Death of JOHN B. HINES, Esq. – We are pained to announce the death of JOHN B. HINES, Esq. which occurred this morning, about eight o'clock. MR. HINES was employed as assistant editor, on two of the papers of this city, during several months of last year. He left Montgomery last fall, and, we believe, has since resided in Charleston, where about four months ago he received terrible injuries by jumping or falling from the window of his room, in escaping from a fire. He partially recovered, however, and came here a few days since to assist in the editorial management of the Messenger. Since his arrival he has been confined, suffering greatly, from his wounds...His age we suppose was about twenty-eight...

Issue of October 14, 1856

Married – On Sunday morning the 5th instant, at the residence of MRS. LUCINDA PEARCE, in Twiggs county, near Marion, by the Rev. LEWIS SOLOMON, WILLIAM H. BECKOM, Esq. to MISS GERALDINE C. SOLOMON, daughter of Col. HENRY SOLOMON, late of said county.

On the 2nd inst. by Rev. SYLVANUS LANDRUM, and at his residence, MR. JOHN G. MARTIN, JR. to MISS FANNIE GAMBLE, all of this city.

In this city, on the 8th inst., by the Rev. J. E. EVINS, MR. G W. STRICKLAND, of Pennsylvania, to MISS LAURA J. TAYLOR, of this city.

Died – Near this city, on the 8th inst., MRS. FRANCIS W. KILPATRICK, aged 27 years, wife of WILLIAM G. KILPATRICK, and daughter of MRS. MARTHA D. MORRIS of this city. MRS. K. leaves a husband who had idolized her for ten years, and four little children...

Issue of October 21, 1856

Death of Col. OLIVER S. BURROUGHS – With sincere regret we announce the death of the above named gentleman, at Bel-Air, near Tallahassee, Fla., on the evening of Saturday, 11th inst. He was accidentally shot by the discharge of his own gun, whilst hunting on Friday, the 10th. In crossing a small water course near Munson's Lake, in company with other gentlemen, both barrels of his gun exploded, the charges entering the lower part of his right arm near the socket, tearing off a part of the shoulder bone, and leaving the wadding and eight shot in the wound. He was very soon carried home, where he lingered until 9 ½ o'clock on Saturday evening, in possession of his faculties to the last.

Col. BURROUGHS was a native of Savannah, where he leaves an only surviving brother. He commanded for a short time the Georgia Hussars, a volunteer cavalry corps of Savannah. His immediate family were a wife and three children.
Georgian Journal

Obituary – JOHN P. BARRON, son of the late WM. & SARAH D. BARRON, was born in Morgan county, Ga., Nov. 15, 1830. He united with the M.E. Church and professed conversion in 1850. Feeling that it was his duty to labor in the Master's Vineyard, he obtained license to exhort. He graduated with distinction at Emory College, July 1851. On August of the same year he became Principal of the Male Academy in Clinton, Ga. (the place which had been his home since the 12th year of his age) in which responsible position he continued to labor until last Fall, when his health became so feeble that he was compelled to relinquish his charge. During the present year continued hemorrhage of the lungs evinced that he was rapidly sinking under Consumption…accompanied by his mother, he went to Philadelphia, where he died in great peace, Sept. 3rd…

Died – In Talbotton, Ga., on the 11th last, MR. AUGUSTUS POU (?), aged 22 (?) years.

Issue of October 28, 1856

Melancholy Suicide – A respectable looking man, apparently about 35 years of age, went to the Lanier House last Sunday night and took lodgings, registering himself as A. J. LOUNSBERRY, Somerville, Tenn. During the night he precipitated himself out of the window of his room in the 3d story and was found dead in the morning. We understand he had been previously stopping at the Floyd House and had exhibited indications of insanity.

Accident to MR. VAN BUREN, New York Oct. 25. Ex-President VAN BUREN was thrown from a wagon today, and one arm broken.

Issue of November 4, 1856

Obituary – Died in Savannah, Ga., on Monday 27th October, 1856, THOMAS W., son of THOS. W. and ARABELLA COLLINS, aged 2 years and 8 months.

Issue of November 18, 1856

Suicide – On Saturday morning last, the 8th instant, the citizens of our place were thrown into consternation by the announcement that a suicide had been committed during the night, in one of those drinking and gambling establishments, where the unwary are so often ensnared and led victims to ruin. DR. H. B. PERKINS of Cuthbert, a most estimable and worthy citizen – brother of Judge PERKINS, came up to this place a day or two before with fifteen hundred dollars in his pocket to pay off a bank note. Unfortunately, he got into one of those sinks of iniquity and destruction, was induced to drink, became intoxicated, and then to the gambling table, where he soon saw his last dollar leave him, and his note unpaid. Driven to desperation, he retired to his room, and in the maddening phrenzy of the moment committed the rash act of self destruction, by cutting the artery of one of his wrists from which the current of life soon made its escape; morning revealed the horrid deed, and aroused to indignation the feelings of the community against men who make themselves the willing instruments of every crime known in the black catalogue, even to death itself.

Death of MR. SPIVEY – MR. ELI SPIVEY, the young gentleman who was shot in Girard on Tuesday of last week, in the reencounter with MR. BLACKMON, died on Thursday morning last of the wounds he received. It is supposed that one of the balls entered the lungs, and his physicians not being able to extract it, (unreadable).

Married – In this city, by Rev. R. L. _ECK, on the 6th inst., HENRY C. BILLUPS, M.D., to MISS EMMA V. CONNELLY, of Burke county.

Died – In Savannah, on the 11th inst., MR. W. D. BULKLEY, formerly of this city, aged 23 years.

Issue of November 25, 1856

Died – Beallwood, near Columbus, on the 21st inst., in the 24th year of her age, MRS. CAROLINE MATILDA, wife of WM. H. GRISWOLD, Junior Proprietor of the Columbus Enquirer, and daughter of DR. L.F.W. ANDREWS of Macon.

Issue of December 2, 1856

Married – On the 27th of November, by Rev. ALEX M. THIGPEN, MR. JOHN W. FINNEY and MISS FRANCES, daughter of JAS. GODDARD, Esq. all of Jones county, Ga.

Issue of December 16, 1856

Dreadful Accident – We learn that a distressing accident happened near Dysarville, McDowell county a few days since. The tressel work being put up by DR. VANDYKE for conveying water for mining purposes, fell, or gave way, instantly killing five white men and seriously wounding seven or eight others, some of whom will probably die. The only names we have heard are those of MR. POTEET and EPLEY, both killed - Ashville, N.C. News, Dec. 4

Married – On the evening of the 9th instant, by Rev. J. L. WARREN, MR. CALEB R. BARRETT and MISS ELIZA RATLIFFE, all of Houston county.

In Crawford county, Dec. 9th, by Rev. WESLEY F. SMITH, MR. JOHN BLOSSENGAME and MISS MARY J. FRUTRILL, all of Crawford.

In Butler, Taylor county, by the same, MR. JULIUS H. HOLSEY, Esq. and MISS MARTHA E. MONTFORT.

On the morning of the 10th inst. by Rev. S. W. DURHAM, MR. WM. H. MONTFORT, of Butler, Ga., to MISS ARABELLA A. COLBERT, of Taylor county.

In Granville, Tenn., by the Hon. D. C. SHEPHERD, on Friday, Nov. 5th, MR. E. J. M. GRACE, OF Georgia to MISS MARY LEE GRACE, of Tennessee.

Issue of December 23, 1856

Died – In this county, on the 10th instant, MR. WILLIAM KILPATRICK, aged 74 years. He was a loving husband, an affectionate father, a kind master...

In this city, of consumption, on Thursday, Dec. 18th, MRS. JULIA KELLY, widow of the late MR. P. KELLY – a native of county Lowth, Ireland. She leaves an only child, PATRICK HENRY KELLY, to mourn his loss.

Married – In Eatonton, Ga., on the 18th inst., by Rev. DR. S. K. TALMAGE, JAMES T. NISBET, Esq., of Macon and MARY SEYMOUR, oldest daughter of JUNIUS WINGFIELD, Esq. of the former place.

On the 18th inst., by Rev. S. LANDRUM, MR. DAVID M. SMITH to MISS ANN E. BAGBY of Bibb county.

Issue of December 30, 1856

Married – December 23d, by Rev. ALEX. M. THIGPEN, MR. LEVI W. JARREL, of Jones county, to MISS MARY C. HARRIS, daughter of Rev. ISAAC C. HARRIS, of Fort Valley, Ga.

Issue of January 6, 1857

Married – In this county, on the 30th inst., by STERLING TUCKER, Esq. ELISHA ERWIN, Esq. of Jones county to MISS REBECCA CHAMBLES, of Bibb county.

On the 4th inst., by Rev. S. LANDRUM, MR. WILLIAM H. SHAW of Americus to MISS MARGARET A. WAGNON of this city.

Died – In Perry, Houston county, Georgia, of Scarlet Fever, on 16th December last, FANNIE COBB, infant daughter of DOCTOR and MRS. P.B.D.H. CULLER.

$300 Reward – Broke out of Clinton jail, on the night of the 31st December last, JOHN NEWTON, who stands charged with the offense of assault with intent to murder. He is about 28 years of age, five feet eleven and a half inches high, blue eyes, fair complexion, freckled face, hair inclined to be red sandy, weight about one hundred and eighty-five pounds, inclined to be bald-headed, and of great muscular appearance. I will pay the above reward for his delivery to me in this place, or of his safe confinement in any jail of this State, so as he can be brought to justice.

JAS. T. RENFROE
Sheriff Jones county, Ga.

Issue of January 13, 1857

More Indian Murders In Florida – Two young men, sons of MR. SHELDON, of Orange county, out on a ducking excursion on the 23d ult., put into shore to the house of a

MR. SHIVE, on Mosquito South Lagoon, four miles south of the settlement of New Smyrna, intending to pass the night with MR. SHIVE and family. To their horror, they found the whole family, consisting of four persons, butchered. Upon subsequent and careful examination, it is supposed that the bloody deed was perpetrated on the 20th. MR. and MRS. SHIVE and one child were shot in the act of escaping and the other child, a cripple, burned with the house. They had but lately removed from Philadelphia to Florida for the purpose of cultivating the orange.

Married – In Jones county, on Thursday, the 8th inst. at the residence of MR. PAUL, by the Rev. JAMES E. EVANS, MR. BENJAMIN F. WILDER to MISS LUCY PAUL of Jones county.

In Wilmington, N.C. on the 6th inst., by the Rev. MR. DRANE, DR. JAMES ARRINGTON MILLER, of Oglethorpe, Georgia and MISS ANN ELIZA, daughter of the Hon. WILLIAM S. ASHE, of the former city.

Died – On Sabbath morning, on the 4th inst., at Brunswick, Ga. after a lingering illness, T. J. COCHRANE aged nineteen, youngest son of Col. ALLEN COCHRANE, of Forsyth...

Died in this city on Monday 5th inst. MR. HARDY MORRIS. He was born in Franklin county, N.C. on 25th of August 1807. He removed to Jones co., Ga. when but four years of age, but had been a resident of this city for about 18 years...He leaves an interesting family of children and a deeply afflicted wife to mourn his unexpected departure...

$50 Reward – Stolen or runaway from the subscriber on the 28th of December, my negro boy MANUEL. Said boy is about 35 years of age, and is a bright mulatto, has a heavy head of hair, and down look, his right foot is deformed, also his right hand – is about 5 feet and 8 inches in height, and will weigh about 150 pounds, by trade a blacksmith. I will pay 50 dollars for the above described boy, and evidence sufficient to convict the person who decoyed him away.

WILLIAM HUCKHABY
Russellville, Monroe co, Ga., Jan. 6, 1857

Issue of January 20, 1857

Man Killed – Strange Coincidence – On last Thursday night as the locomotive "Young America", H. HISER, engineer, was drawing a passenger train from Rochester to Aburn, a man who resided in Victor was discovered lying on the track, two miles west of the station. He was discovered too late to save his life. The locomotive struck him, passed over his body, and left scarcely enough of it in its natural condition to enable it to be recognized as that of a human being. The engine was stopped as soon as possible and the remains taken to Victor.

A Drummer's Funeral – OLD ALBERT, the Drummer, was buried with all the honors last Wednesday. A formidable array of colored Musicians, bearing their instruments in mourning draped, led the sable procession – drums and fifes preceded the hearse playing a melancholy strain, and a long train of the colored population on foot and in carriages, brought up the rear…OLD ALBERT, or as he used to style himself, ALBERT COLLINS, was an old resident of Macon…ALBERT was pretty much his own man, and did as he pleased. For some time past, he has been a member of the Presbyterian Church, and died in peace and cheerfulness…

Married – In this city on the 13th inst., by Rev. R. L. BRECK, J. HARRIS, Esq. of Thomasville, to MISS MARY C. WILEY.

Also, on the 13th inst., by the same, Hon. CLIFFORD ANDERSON to MISS ANNA C. LECONTE.

Died – In the Warrior District, on the 9th inst., of Pneumonia, PETER B. MCCREADY.

Issue of January 27, 1857

Died – At Palatka, Florida, on Monday the 22nd December, 1856, of consumption, FRANCIS W. MACARTHY, a citizen of Macon, Ga.

Issue of February 3, 1857

Congress – The death and obsequies of Hon. PRESTON S. BROOKS constituted a melancholy and startling episode in the Congressional record last week.

Death of JOHN BARNEY – Washington, Jan. 25 – That old citizen, whose pen has of late been employed in the pleasant occupation of character painting from the great men of the Revolution, and of late periods, died today of pneumonia. His sketches of AARON BURR and others, which he had permitted to preceded the publication of his complete work, are still going the rounds of the press, almost fresh from his pen.

Married – On Monday Feb. 2nd, 1857, at the Baptist Church, by the Rev. S. LANDRUM, MR. JOEL P. CALLOWAY, to MISS LOU ELLIS, daughter of WM. ELLIS, Esq. all of the City of Macon.

Died, in this city on Saturday January 24th, 1857 SARAH SOPHIA, only daughter of MR. CHARLES and MRS. SOPHIA F. COLLINS, aged 12 years, 8 months and 4 days.

Issue of February 10, 1857

New York Negroes in Slavery – New York, Feb 2. Gov. KING has sent a message to the Legislature, respecting two colored citizens of New York, who are held in slavery in the South. One of them is named HENRY DIXON, and was sold to MR. DEAN, of Macon, Georgia.

Murder – The Forsyth Educational Journal of the 21st ult., says that two young men by the name of SIMMONS and BRYAN, from Monroe county, went to Philadelphia, a few months ago, to attend a course of Medical Lectures. They were rooming together, and got into a serious disagreement, upon which a pistol was discharged. Some persons in the street hearing the report, and fearing something serious had occurred, forced their way into the room, and found young SIMMONS shot through, of which wound he died in two or three days. MR. BRYAN escaped, and up to last accounts had not been arrested. Empire State.

Fatal Affray – A fight took place on Saturday, 31st Jan. at the Columbus Factory two miles above the city, between THOMAS OLIVER and DR. ADAM FLOYD, in which FLOYD was shot through the right side and will probably die. OLIVER delivered himself up to the officer of the law.

Married – In Livingston, on the evening of the 15th inst., by the Rev. JOHN GARRETT, MR. O T. GRACE, of Granville, to MISS DELILAH GARRETT, of Livingston, Overton county Tenn.

On the 28th ult., by Rev. MR. HINTON, Rev. J. P. DUNCAN, of the Georgia Conference, to MRS. S.H.DANIEL, of Americus.

Issue of February 17, 1857

Ferocious Assault upon an Editor – Middletown, (Con.) Feb 9 – WALTER S. CARTER, editor of the Middlesex country Argus, was severely beaten here this morning by Capt. JAMES DEKAY, in consequence of an article in his paper reflecting severely upon Rev. E. HARWOOD, MRS. HARWOOD, and her sister, MISS DEKAY. MR. CARTER is bleeding freely at the lungs and his recovery is considered doubtful.

Sad Case – One of the most respected and beloved preachers of the Gospel in Montgomery, who has for some time shown symptoms of approaching insanity, has at length become a confirmed lunatic, and has been conveyed to an asylum. It is altogether a distressing case, but we do not feel at liberty to enter into particulars. We learn through a private source, that the person alluded to is the Rev. DAVID FINDLEY, for many years the pastor of the Presbyterian Church in that city.

Died – On the 7th inst., at his residence in Houston county, Georgia, DR. CREED TAYLOR WOODSON, in the 56th year of his age.

Capt. WILLIAM MANERS, we are grieved to learn, says the Texas Advocate, of 31st Jan. died of pneumonia in Houston on Thursday night of last week…He was an old Texan, an honest and a good Christian. He had for many long years been a devoted member of the Methodist Church. Capt. MANERS was a native of S.C. where he leaves many relatives, and was well known in Florida, where he resided several years.

Probable Death of DR. KANE – Philadelphia, Feb. 17th – Judge KANE of this city has received advices from Havana, that induces the belief that his relative, DR. KANE, the arctic explorer is dead.

Issue of March 3, 1857

Another Fatal Duel – We regret to record the repetition of an occurrence by which our community was so shocked but a week ago. Another hostile meeting took place yesterday near this city, in which the parties were O.S. KIMBROUGH and JACOB P. HENDRICK, both citizens of Columbus, in this state. The weapons used were rifles and they fought at forty paces distance. Upon the second fire MR. HENDRICK fell, mortally wounded, the ball having entered his side just above the hip and passed, it is thought, through the smaller intestines. He was brought to this city, and was alive at a late hour last night, though his condition is considered hopeless. His antagonist escaped unhurt and left for Columbus by the evening train. Sav. Rep. 24th
MR. JACOB P. HENDRICK, the gentleman referred to in the above, was a native of this city, and his mother, sister and brother reside in Hamburg. A telegraph dispatch from Savannah states that he died from the effect of his wound yesterday morning about six o'clock.

Married – In this city, on the 27th Feb. by Rev. SYLVANUS LANDRUM, DR. JAMES J. PARKS, of Albany and MISS P. MARY J. STEWART of this city.

Hand the Scoundrel Around – Absconded from the City of Macon, on Wednesday night the 5th inst., a man by the name of GEORGE A. SMITH, a name no doubt, which he has assumed. He is about forty years old, fair complexion, auburn hair, hazle eyes, one of his front teeth out, and a scar upon one of his wrists. The above described scoundrel and imposter by false pretension and representation, imposed himself upon a very respectable but unsuspecting young lady in Macon county, Ga., and married her; and leaving under the pretense of going with her to Missouri, he deserted her in the City of Macon, having converted all her property into money. I am under the impression that this is not the only offence of the kind, consequently I take this method of warning the country at large against the scoundrel.

JOHN W. MARTIN

Issue of March 17, 1857

Duel at Washington – THOS. J. MUNDAY and DR. BRADFORD, both of New York, in consequence of an affray at one of the principal hotels on Saturday night, fought a duel near Washington City on Sunday afternoon. Two shots were fired, neither party being injured, and the affair was then amicably adjusted.

Married – In Vineville, on the 10th inst., by the Rev. MR. EVANS, P. TRACY, Esq. (former editor of this paper) and CAROLINE M. WALKER, daughter of the late JOHN RAWLS.

Issue of March 31, 1857

University of Georgia – Hon. L. M. KEIT will deliver the annual address this year before the societies at the University of Georgia.

Married – On the morning 22d inst., by Rev. LEWIS SOLOMON, TROY G. HOLDEN, Esq. to MISS MARY A. F. BARTON, all of Twiggs county, Ga.

Issue of April 7, 1857

Married – On the evening of the 31st March, at the residence of MR. SAM'L MCARTHUR, by the Rev. SAM'L B. BURNETT, MR. JOHN J. RILEY and MISS SARAH A. NEEL, of Bibb.

Died – In this city, on Wednesday evening last, MR. WM. B. WATTS aged about 50 years, an old resident of Macon.

Death of SAMPSON W. HARRIS – We regret to learn from the dispatches received here yesterday, the death at Washington City, of S. W. HARRIS, Esq. late representative of the 3d Congressional District and more recently of the 9th District. He has been in Congress, we believe, for four terms. He was a gentleman of fair ability, amiable and gentlemanly n his dispositions. His early decease will be mourned in sincere sorrow by many personal friends.

Issue of April 14, 1857

Col. LANE, of Kansas notoriety, is married again, his former wife from whom he had been divorced, being his wife.

Obituary –MRS. JANE DAY, wife of Hon. JOSEPH DAY, died in Houston county on April 7th. She was born in Richmond co., and was the daughter of NEHEMIAH and ANN DUNN. She was a member of the Methodist Church and lived a Christian during fifty years. She lived three score and ten on the earth.

Issue of April 21, 1857

Funeral Invitations – The friends and acquaintances of MR. E.C. GRISWOLD, deceased, are requested to attend his funeral, from his late residence in Vineville, this morning, at half past 10 o'clock.

Issue of April 28, 1857

Married – In Twiggs co., by the Rev. C.A. THARP, on the evening of the 21st of April, 1857, MR. ACTON E. NASH to

MISS ROIXEY ANN CHAPPEL, daughter of T. S. CHAPPELL, all of the above co.

On Tuesday, the 21st inst., at 11 o'clock, by RICHARD HUTCHERSON, Esq., MISS MARTHA C. MAULDIN, of Upson county, Ga. and THEOPHILUS J. HARDISON, of Houston county, Ga.

Issue of May 5, 1857

Drowned – On Saturday last, the 15th inst., the body of a man named EZRA ROOT was discovered in the Ocklocknee River about fourteen miles above Thomasville. A horse and buggy belonging to the deceased were also discovered at the same time, horse likewise drowned. A Coroner's Jury was summoned and a post mortem examination held on Saturday evening when it was pronounced that deceased came to his death by drowning. It is supposed that deceased was drowned on Tuesday previous to his discovery on Saturday, and in a state of intoxication at the time. He was known to several of out citizens as a resident of Barnesville, Pike county, Georgia, formerly from Suffield in the State of Maine, but latterly a traveling cigar agent. Enterprise.

Shocking Accident at Suspension Bridge – We learn that a man named CHUBRICK, residing at Niagara City, walked off the bank of the river at Suspension Bridge, on the Canada side, last Saturday night. He had been engaged in moving a building on the Canada side, and was on his way homeward, somewhat intoxicated, when, mistaking a light for that on the bridge, he walked off the precipice and fell a distance of one hundred and fifty feet, striking the rocks below, and breaking almost every bone in his body. Buffalo Commercial.

Died – In Crawford county, on the 27th inst., JAMES AVERA, in the 59th year of his age. MR. AVERA had been a citizen of Crawford county for the last thirty years. He was a good neighbor, a kind father and an affectionate husband.

Issue of May 12, 1857

Married – On Tuesday the 5th inst., by the Rev. SAMUEL B. BURNETT, MR. WM.J. SLOCUMB to MISS VICTORIA E. WILLIAMSON, all of Crawford co., Ga.

Died – In Pulaski county, April 28th, 1857, in the forty-eighth year of her age, MRS. ELIZABETH BOOTHE, wife of THEOPHILUS D. BOOTHE, and daughter of MR. JAMES PHILLIPS. The subject of this brief obituary died in Houston county, near Fort Valley, May 2d – age 21.

HENRY HARRIS, a kind and affectionate son, brother and pupil, has left us for a home in Heaven.

Issue of May 19, 1857

Married – At the residence of P. W. GRAY of Houston county, on the 11th inst., by Judge C. D. ANDREWS, MR. W. A. ANSLEY, of Crawford county, and MISS SARAH CHEEVES of Macon county, Ga.

Obituary - MRS. NANCY ANN HALL, wife of M. W. HALL, Esq. of Houston county, died in that county on the 1st instant, of Puerpal Fever, after an illness of fourteen days, during which she suffered great bodily pain...She has left husband, a tender babe and affectionate friends to mourn her loss.

Near Macon on the 6th inst., MRS. SUSAN KING, in the 73d year of her age.

In Hawkinsville, Ga. on Friday evening, the 8th inst., EMILY L. GRACE, a daughter of SAMUEL and NANCY

M. GRACE and wife of MATTHEW GRACE, Esq., aged thirty two years two months and twenty five days.

Issue of May 26, 1857

A Negro Elected to Office – THOMAS HOWLAND, a Negro stevedore, has been elected warden in the third ward of Providence, R.I. The result, it appears, was brought about through a joke, but it turned out to be a reality, and a few days ago HOWLAND demanded to be sworn into office. His election, upon examination, was found to be legal, and he was thereupon sworn, and entered upon the discharge of his duties.

Murder in Brunswick – A brutal murder was committed in Brunswick, Ga., on the evening of the 16th by CHAS. MOORE, City Marshal, upon the person of J.R. WOOD, Keeper of the Oglethorpe House. An altercation had taken place during the day in relation to MOORE's chastisement of one of WOOD's servants. In the evening MOORE confronted WOOD, with the remark that he was armed and ready for him. WOOD replied very pleasantly that he had nothing against him, and thereupon was shot dead by MOORE. MOORE then fled. A reward of $1,000 was offered for his apprehension by the Mayor of Brunswick; and we learn by the Savannah Republican that he was taken in Centreville, in Camden county, on his way to Florida, and lodged in Chatham county jail, on the 20th instant, there being no secure place of confinement in Glynn. A feeling of great exasperation against MOORE exists among the people of Brunswick. WOOD was a worthy and quiet man, and has left a widow and young children.

Married – In Madison, on the 20th inst., by the Rev. JAS. L. PIERCE, Rev. JOSHUA KNOWLES, Editor of the Macon Journal & Messenger, to MISS SALLIE E. ROBERTS.

Issue of June 2, 1857

Human Calculation Uncertain – A MRS. FLYNN jumped over the bank of Niagara River, a few days ago, thinking thereby to have escaped this world of trouble. But alas! For woman's calculations, she struck in the top of a tree, after a sail of about one hundred feet in mid air, whence she fell, only bruised and scratched a little, to the ground. She was found on the brink, cogitating over the uncertainty of sublunary things. Exchange.

Married – In Eatonton, May 27, by Rev. E. P. BIRCH, Rev. ALEX. M. THIGPEN, of the Georgia Conference, to MISS JANE M. daughter of C. R. THOMAS, Esq.

Issue of June 9, 1857

The Richmond Enquirer says that about three years ago, MISS ANNE W. TALIAFERRO, of King William county, Va. emancipated 40 negroes, giving each $150. They were placed in a quaker settlement in Ohio, by E. W. SCOTT executor of the estate. A few weeks since MR. SCOTT had occasion to visit them on business, and found them in a wretched condition, almost starving. One of the children had been stolen, and several had died for want of attention and the necessaries of life. They begged MR. SCOTT to allow them to return with him to Virginia and go into slavery.

Died – In this place on the 19th & 21st inst., of Typhoid Dysentery, little CHARLIE and JAMES, only children of J. F. & N. SIKES; the former two, and the latter between four and five years of age.

Issue of June 23, 1857

Obituary – Died, at his residence, in this county, on the 13th inst., RANDOLPH M. GILBERT, aged 54 years. He has left a wife and large family of children...

On the 16th instant, at his residence in Houston county, Ga. the Hon. HENRY GLOVER, in the 76th year of his age.

Issue of June 30, 1857

Died – At Buffalo, N.Y. on the 22d inst., MR. JESSE STONE, formerly a resident of this city, aged 68 years.

$300 Reward – Ranaway from the subscriber, on Saturday night, the 20th day of June, the following described three negro men, to wit: BOB, about 26 years of age, of a yellow complexion, with long curled hair, a little stooped in the shoulders, about 5 feet 9 or 10 inches high, and weighs about 170 pounds. The subscriber purchased BOB from a gentleman of the name of JOHN A. ADDISON, of Edgefield District, South Carolina, some time last winter. BOB was raised near Edgefield Court House. MONTGOMERY is about 28 years of age, of a brown complexion, about 5 feet 9 or 10 inches high, weighs about 170 pounds, is straight built, and has a scar across the instep of one of his feet, made by an axe. And JOE about 22 or 23 years of age, of dark complexion, straight built, eyes full, mouth large, a little hard of hearing, about 5 feet 2 inches high and weighs about 160 pounds. If said negroes have been stolen, I will pay Three Hundred Dollars for the apprehension of the negroes and thief, and their confinement in some safe jail, with ample proof to convict the thief of having stolen said negroes. But if not stolen, I will then pay liberal reward to any one who may apprehend the said three negroes and confine them in some safe Jail so that I may get them. Address me at Lumpkin, Stewart co., Ga.   WILLIAM WEST

$50 Reward – Will be paid for the apprehension of my man PETER, sometimes called JULY, who absconded from plantation in Monroe county in February 1856. PETER is small and quite black, weighs 115 or 120, is lame in the left foot, from being burned and has but little intelligence. From what I have been able to hear of him, he is attempting to get down the Central Rail Road to Savannah, thence to Charleston, from which place he was brought several years ago.

L. N. WHITTLE

Issue of July 7, 1857

Ranaway – From the subscriber in January 1856, my negro man SOL, aged about 25 years, straight and elegantly formed for a negro – prominent eyes and teeth – intelligent and fine looking. A reward of Fifty dollars is offered for his capture. He travels from Macon to Atlanta often, I understand, and stops at Griffin, Barnesville and in the neighborhood of Colaparchee.

A. P. POWERS

Issue of July 14, 1857

Melancholy Affair – Out city was yesterday the scene of intense excitement, occasioned by a street rencounter between MESSRS. NEWMAN MCBAIN and CHARLES W. HANCOCK on one side and MESSRS. HARVEY W. and WILLIAM SHAW, on the other, in which H.W. SHAW was killed. He was wounded by a gun or pistol shot, in the right side, and survived not longer than one hour. WILLIAM SHAW was slightly wounded. Four shots were fired with double barreled guns, two by MCBAIN and two by WM. SHAW. There is some confusion in the statements of the particulars, though there were many persons present at the time. The difficulty was not unexpected, as

there had been a quarrel between the parties some two hours before. The rencounter took place just about noon. We forbear making any comments as the occurrence will probably undergo legal investigation.
Southwestern News

The Death of Hon. WM. L. MARCY is a melancholy event of the last week. He died at Ballston, New York, very suddenly, as is supposed of an affection of the heart, on Saturday, the 4th of July. He had retired to his room at 12 M., slightly indisposed, and was found a few minutes after, dead upon his couch, where he had laid down, after pulling off his boots and putting on slippers. A book he had taken to read was lying upon his breast, and no discomposure of his person or garments, or distortion of face, indicated a death struggle. He must have passed away instantaneously without a moment's warning. MR. MARCY was a native of Massachusetts, born at Sturbridge (now Southbridge) in 1786, and was 71 years of age. He was a volunteer in the War of 1812 – commenced official life as Recorder of Troy in 1818 – was on the State Supreme Bench in '29 and in the same year elevated to the U.S. Senate. He was elected Governor of New York very shortly after and subsequently in State service as Governor and Comptroller, and in the United States service as Secretary of War and of State has achieved for himself a reputation for a wise and sagacious statesmanship rarely excelled.

$30 Reward – Ranaway from the subscriber, on Monday the 6th inst., my man JIM a mulatto, about five feet seven – weighs about 145 pounds – defective front teeth – with a slight lisp. The above reward for his delivery in some safe jail where I can get him, or delivered to me in Macon.

I. C. PLANT

Married – On the evening of the 8th inst., at the house of Capt. DAVID FLANDERS, by the Rev. J. E. EVANS, MR. DANIEL H. ADAMS to MISS HELEN A. SNOW, all of East Macon, Ga.

Issue of July 21, 1857

$75 Reward – Ranaway from the subscriber, during the past year, by boy GREEN, or as some call him, GREEN BERRY; he is young (from 23 to 28 years old) of common height, well made, and very likely, a round head and face, and dark complexion, had ear-rings on, has a scar upon his leg, and I think one upon his forehead or face. He has a father at Griswoldville, a mother at a woman's in Black Ankle, named WEST, and brothers and sisters in the Davis and Andrews settlements. It is supposed he is harbored by his relations and may be by some low white man. I will give seventy-five dollars for his delivery in some safe jail, uninjured in any way, so that I can get him; and if a white man is the harborer, I will pay an hundred dollars for his safe lodgement and proof sufficient to convict him. I hope the people will be vigilant and apprehend him.

       E. F. HAY
       Long Street, Ga.

Married – On the 16th inst., by Hon. G. P. CULVERHOUSE, GEO. M. BAZEMORE to MISS RACHIEL JOHNSON, all of Crawford county, Ga.

Fatal Quarrel Between Politicians – Cincinnati July 11 – The Enquirer learns that a quarrel recently took place in Morgan county, Ky. Between MR. MASON, Democrat, and MR. COX, American, candidates for Congress. The latter was shot by MR. MASON and killed. MR. COX was the late member of Congress from the 9th District. MR. MASON also represented the same district.

Issue of July 28, 1857

Obituary – Died, at her late residence in Bibb county, Ga. on the 19th day of July 1857, of Typhoid Fever, MRS. ELIZABETH THARP, in the 69th year of her age...She has left a large family of children and numerous friends...

Issue of August 11, 1857

MR. DOBBIN, late Secretary of the Navy under MR. PIERCE, expired at Fayetteville, N.C. on the 4th inst., after a protracted illness...He died at the early age of 44...

Died – Of Typhoid Fever, on the 11th of July, 1857, at the residence of her father in Bibb county, Ga., MISS MARTHA A. BAZEMORE, in the 23d year of her age.

OLIVER FLETCHER, infant of OLIVER G. & M. A. EVANS, August 1st, 1857.

In this city, on the 1st inst., PETER ALONZO, infant son of JOHN F. and GEORGIA ANN ARNOLD, Age 2 years and 3 months.

$50 Reward – A negro man, a slave, named FRANK, usually goes by the name FRANK PEPPER, ranaway from the subscriber on the 25th inst. The above reward will be given to any one who will deliver said negro to me or safely lodge him in the jail in Macon, or in any jail in this State, by immediately notifying me of the fact. FRANK is a dark mulatto, has a bushy head of hair, rather quick spoken, can read and write, (spells badly and may have a pass of his own writing), he is rather medium size. He may attempt to escape to a free state and all ship masters, R. Road conductors and Marshals of towns and cities are solicited to keep a look out for him.

SAMUEL GRISWOLD

Issue of August 18, 1857

Suicide of Gen. RUSK – Gen. RUSK has, ever since the death of his wife, suffered under a mental depression which at times bore him down beneath its weight. He has to a great extent, secluded himself from society, and lately that despondency has been more marked and apparent to those familiar with him. A severe illness from which he was just recovering, had prostrated him for weeks, and he was suffering greatly from a rising back of his neck.
On yesterday evening, about 2 o'clock, his family hearing the report of a gun and the fall of a body, ran to the spot, and found him lying dead upon the ground, behind the gallery at the back of the house, with a rifle under him. A coroner's jury was summoned, from whose verdict we extract the following: "The cause of his death was a gunshot (rifle) wound on the fore part of his head, inflicted from a rifle gun, held in his own hands and discharged by himself."

Issue of September 1, 1857

Died – In this city, June 22d, of Typhoid Fever, MRS. MALINDA, wife of F. M. ALLEY, aged 23 years and 9 months.

Also, on the 18th ult., HOWELL COBB, infant son of the above. Aged 1 year and 8 days.

Issue of September 8, 1857

Obituary – Died, near this city, on the morning of the 24th ultimo, after a short illness, MRS. FRANCES M. GREER, wife of E. C. GREER, Esq. and daughter of the Hon. WASHINGTON POE. She was for a number of years a member of the Presbyterian Church in this city.

Died, in Lowndes county, after a long and protracted illness, FANNY, the youngest daughter of E. and OPHELIA DUMUND. Aged one year and seven months.

In Crawford county, Ga. at his residence, after a short illness, JOHN STEMBRIDGE, in his sixty- seventh year. He was interred with Masonic ceremonies...

Married – On the morning of the 3d inst., by Rev. LEWIS SOLOMON, at the residence of WM. S. KELLY, Esq. (Twiggs county) HENRY H. COX, Esq. of Clinton, Ga. to MISS MARY VIRGINIA WILLIAMS, daughter of Col. WILLIAM WILLIAMS of the city of Brunswick, Ga.

Issue of September 15, 1857

Runaway –About the first of April, my Negro Man named DENNIS about 36 years old, dark complected. The said negro ranaway from MR. HARDY PERKINS of Munroe county, and I purchased him of MR. PERKINS as he run. I will give Twenty Dollars to any person that will deliver said Negro to me or lodge him in any Jail, so I can get him.
J. HOLLINGSWORTH

Melancholy Occurrence – We are sorry to learn in the annexed paragraph from a Jacksonville (Florida) paper, the death of a highly intelligent, accomplished gentleman, with whom we were personally acquainted. DR. SPEER was a brother of Col. A. M. SPEER, of this city, and a son of Rev. A. SPEER, of LaGrange. He was widely known in Florida, had been for several years a member of the General Assembly and sustained in all his relations an elevated and irreproachable character.
We learn from a passenger by the steamer Welaka, arrived Saturday, that on Wednesday last as DR. SPEAR, a wealthy planter of Lake Monroe, was having a small steamer which he built for his private use, towed by the steamer Darlington to Jacksonville for repairs, his vessel

was sunk, and he and one of his negroes was drowned, the particulars of which, as related, were as follows: While in tow in the middle of Lake George, the small steamer badly leaking, was suddenly swamped by the heavy sea running at the time. DR. SPEAR, his son, (a lad), P. EVERLETT, and a negro, were on board at the time of her sinking. MR. EVERLETT was rescued by a boat from the Darlington; DR. S's son was saved by clinging to a floating box from which he was taken on board the boat. DR. SPEER and his negro sunk. It is supposed that in making an effort to save the negro, the latter drowning, clung to the Dr. (who was an excellent swimmer) in such a manner as to disable him entirely from keeping above water, until the boat reached them. Capt. BROCK of the Darlington, made every effort to recover the bodies, but in vain.

DR. S's lady – a daughter of Col. I.D. HART, of Jacksonville, Fla. And children, are now at their residence on Lake Monroe, and will not hear of the melancholy tidings until Tuesday of this week.

Died, In this city, on the 19th August, MR. LEONARD W. GIBSON, formerly of England, of Bilious Intermittent Fever. Aged 55 years.

Died, at his residence in Jones county, Sept. 4th, of a bilious affection, GEORGE W. CALDWELL, only child of ROBT. CALDWELL.

Died, in Dougherty county, near Albany, July 25th, at the residence of GILES D. BEARDIN, LEARY C. infant son of ROBERT M. and TEMPERANCE LILLY. Aged eleven months and nineteen days.

Died, in the city of Mobile, Ala., on the 2d of July last, MRS. LUCY B. wife of THOS. A. HAMILTON, Esq. She was a member of the Presbyterian Church.

Issue of September 22, 1857

Obituary – Died, in Knoxville, Crawford county, Ga., on Saturday, September 12th, 1857, aged 33 years, MRS. REBECA JANE ANDREWS, wife of THOMAS ANDREWS, and daughter of JOHN and MARTHA SIMMONS. MRS. ANDREWS joined the M.E. Church in 1827...

Issue of September 29, 1857

Obituary – Died, at the residence of his Grandmother, MRS. BARBEE, in Jasper county, on the 14th instant, ABNER HAYNE, only son of STEPHEN W. and SARAH F. PARKER, of Colquitt, Miller county, Ga. Aged one year, one month and twenty days.

Death of an Editor – Major JOHN C. BATES, editor of the Montgomery Journal, died on Tuesday, at the residence of the late Major COWLES, four miles from this city. Major BATES was born in Vermont and came south in 1839. He married the daughter of Gen. TALIFAFERRO, on Montgomery, where he has been connected with the Journal for 15 years. He was 45 years of age.

Our readers generally will be shocked at the announcement of the death of Judge DRYSDALE, who died at his residence in this city yesterday afternoon. His funeral will take place at 4 o'clock this afternoon. Savannah Georgian

Issue of October 5, 1857

Died, In this city, Sept. 27th, MATTIE, youngest daughter of DR. and MRS. ROBT. COLLINS, aged 2 years and 8 months, after a brief illness of congestion of the brain...

Issue of October 13, 1857

Baltimore, Oct. 8 – The Hon. LOUIS MCLANE died in this city yesterday.

Tribute of Respect to the Memory of Lt. WM. L. HERNDON.

Issue of October 20, 1857

Died, In Marshallville, Macon county, Ga., on the 2d inst. of Pulmonary disease, MARY JANE, wife of C. W. NIXON and daughter of the late SOLOMON FUDGE of Houston. Aged twenty-four years. She leaves a large circle of friends and two young children to mourn her.

Issue of October 27, 1857

Married – In Griffin, on Tuesday the 20th inst., at the residence of Judge J.P. REID, by the Rev. C.P.B. MARTIN, EMORY WINSHIP, Esq. of this city, to MISS LIZZIE ALEXANDER, of the former place.

Ten Dollars Reward – Ranaway from the subscriber, about three weeks since, his negro woman ELIZA, about 40 years of age, of yellowish complexion, about 5 feet six or eight inches high. The above reward will be paid for her apprehension and delivery to the undersigned in Macon.

THOS. B. ARTOPE

Died, In this city on Wednesday morning 14th inst., of Typhoid Bilious Fever, A. LOUISA, second daughter of A.K. and E. W. MCLAUGHLIN, aged 21 years.

Ranaway – About the 25th Sept. last, my man STEPHEN, about forty years old, copper colored, front teeth out and sometimes stammers in talking – he is about five feet six inches high, has acquaintances that may no doubt harbor him near Pinter Town, Worth co., also about Fort Valley. I will give Ten Dollars for his apprehension and delivery to me in Perry, and Fifty Dollars for proof to conviction of his being harbored by a white person while runaway.

W. F. POSTELL

Issue of November 10, 1857

An affray, we are told, occurred at a "Corn Shucking" last Saturday night week, at Nelson's Place, near this city, between WM. HOLT and GEORGE KNIGHT, in which the former was severely cut in several places and died yesterday morning. KNIGHT has been committed to answer.

The Rev. D. J. AULD, of the Presbyterian Church, died in Tallahassee, Florida, on the 30th ult.

Died, In Bibb county, Oct. 28th after a brief illness of Croup, CHARLIE I., son of WM. and LOUISA JOHNSON, aged six years and three months.

Issue of November 17, 1857

MR. KENAN, of Baldwin, on the 12th, announced in the House the death of Hon. DUNCAN J. DAVIS, a representative from Early county, who died suddenly of pneumonia. His remains were followed by the Legislature to the Railway station, and a committee of two from each House accompanied them home.

Death of MRS. RUSH – This accomplished and hospitable lady of Philadelphia, whose name is familiar in every circle in the United States as a social leader, died at Saratoga on the 23d ult. The poor as well as the fashionable will mourn her death.

Died, in Houston county, on the 9th inst., JOHN SAMUEL, son of DR. EDMUND J. MCGEHEE, aged fourteen years eleven months and twenty-one days. His disease was catarrh and inflammation of the brain.

Death of a Tallahassee Merchant – We regret to have to chronicle the death of another of our citizens in the person of FREDERICK TOWLE of the firm of Towle and Myers of this city. He died in New York, on the 29th October, of inward rheumatism – a disease with which he had long been afflicted. MR. T. was a native of New Hampshire, but had resided in this city since 1827, during the most of which time he had been engaged in business as a Silver Smith...He died in the communion of the Presbyterian Church, (having been converted under the preaching of the Rev. DR. HOYT, of Athens, Ga. during a visit of that distinguished divine to this city in 1843)...He leaves no family, having never been married. His age was about sixty.   Floridian

A Tribute of Respect – JOSEPH B. CRAWFORD

Killed at Warrenton – We learn that a boy named WHITESIDES, shot and killed JOHN JENNINGS last Friday night. It appears that a quarrel occurred between JENNINGS and the father of young WHITESIDES, during which JENNINGS drew a pistol and snapped it twice at the old man. Before he made his third attempt the boy seized a shotgun, and discharged the contents into JENNINGS side, inflicting a mortal wound. Augusta Dispatch

Married, By Rev. LEWIS SOLOMON, on the morning of the 22d inst. HENRY LOYLESS, Esq. to MISS MARTHA LAND, daughter of HENRY LAND, all of Twiggs co., Ga.

Issue of December 8, 1857

Married, In Wilkinson county, on the evening of the 12th ult., by the Rev. G. R. MCCALL, Col. E. TRESSILLIAN

NAPIER of Macon, to MISS EUGENIE CARSWELL, daughter of W. E. CARSWELL, Esq. of Wilkinson.

In Monroe county, on the 24th ult., in the morning, at the residence of MRS. HOLLIS, by the Rev. DAVIS SMITH, Col. K.L. WORTHY, of Hickory Grove, Crawford county, to MISS LIZZIE BOZEMAN.

Also, at the same time and place, THOS. J. SIMMONS, Esq. of Knoxville, Ga. to MISS PENNIE HOLLIS.

Died, In Vineville on the 2d, inst., at an advanced age MRS. CHLOE N. KELSEY, widow of the late Capt. NOAH KELSEY, formerly of Powelton, Georgia.

Issue of December 15, 1857

Death of an old Printer – SAMUEL WRIGHT MINOR, probably the oldest printer in Georgia, died in this city, last Thursday, after a lingering illness of three months. He was born in Queen Anne's county, Maryland, in the year 1781, and removed to Georgia early in life. He served an apprentice in the office of WILLIAM J. BUNEE of Augusta...He was the son of Col. WILLIAM MINOR, an officer in Revolutionary Army, and though not a member of any branch of the Christian Church, gave ample assurance that he died in peace with God and man.

Issue of December 22, 1857

Death of J. MILTON CLAPP – The Charleston Mercury of the 17th comes to us in mourning for the death of J. MILTON CLAPP, Esq. so long one of the able editors of that paper. He was a native of Ohio, and died in the 48th year of his age.

Married – On the night of 1st December, by the Rev. CHARLES R. JEWETT in the city of Griffin, Ga. DR. J.

HENRY CONNALLY of Barnesville, Ga. and MISS BENIE M. FREEMAN, of the former place.

In this city, on the 16th inst., by Rev. J. KNOWLES, Rev. WILLIAM F. COOK of the Georgia Conference, to MISS LOU. J. daughter of ALEX. RICHARDS, Esq.

INDEX

A

A. Louisa	157
Abanatha, Mr. W. A.	31
Abe	101, 102
Abner Hayne	156
Abrams, Jacob L.	26
Abrum	46
Acker, Mr.	64
Acker, Mr. George W.	64
Adam	46
Adams, Geo. W.	113
Adams, John Quincy	23
Adams, Mr. Daniel H.	151
Addison, Andrew J.	15
Addison, John A.	148
aeronaut	19, 92
Agee, Dr.	109
Albert	37, 96, 137
Albert D.	37
Aldridge, Miss Henrietta	35
Alexander, Miss Lizzie	157
Alfred	42, 128
Allby, F. H.	86
Allen	124
Allen, Miss	124
Alley, F. H.	49
Alley, F. M.	153
Alley, Mrs.	49
Anderson	13, 90
Anderson, Hon. Clifford	138
Anderson, James	90
Andrews, Bishop	39
Andrews, D. E.	83
Andrews, J. H.	107

Andrews, Judge C. D. 145
Andrews, Mrs. 156
Andrews, Mrs. Rebeca Jane 156
Andrews, Thomas 156
Anghe, Mr. John 20
Ann 18, 72, 84, 152
Ann Eliza, Miss 111, 136
Ann Maria 72
Ansley 18
Ansley, Mr. W. A. 145
Arban, M. 19
Archer 59
Archer, Wm. A. 59
Armstrong, Gen. 23
Arnow, Joshua J. 105
Arthur, Miss Margiania 46
Artope, J. B. 119
Artope, Thos. B. 157
Ashe, Hon. William S. 136
Atkinson, Rev. W. Y. 40
Attoway 59
Attoway, J. 59
Auld, Rev. D. J. 158
Avera, James 144
Avera, Mr. 144
Averett, DR. 77

B

B., Mr. 62, 77
Babbitt, Mr. C. A. 33
Bagby, Miss Ann E. 134
Baily, Hon. John 14
Baird, Rev. Mr. 16
Baja, John 39
Baker 69, 96, 121
Baker, James 69
Baker, William 121

Balch, Mr. 34
Balch, Mr. Joseph 34
Baldridge, Dr. Joseph H. 114
Baldwin, John 49
Bandy, Miss Mary 54
Bandy, Mr. Wm. C. 83
Banks, George 105
Barbee, Mrs. 156
Barber, Captain 21
Barberee 126
Barberee, Stansell 126
Barbour, John S. Sr. 63
Barlow, Billy 125
Barnes 91
Barnes, James G. 11, 31
Barney, John 138
Barrett, Mr. Caleb R. 133
Barron, John P. 131
Barron, Mr. Robert H. 99
Barron, Wm. and Sarah D. 131
Barry, Hon. William T. 55
Barry, M. V. 80
Barton, Miss Mary A. F. 142
Bass, Mary 37
Bass, Miss Tempy E. 37
Bassett, Rev. J. 102
Bateman, Mrs. Charity 86
Bateman, Seaborn M. and Ruth 87
Bates, Major 156
Bates, Major John C. 156
Baxter, Thomas W. 58
Bazemore, Geo. M. 151
Bazemore, Miss Martha A. 152
Beale, Stephen J. 54
Beardin, Giles D. 155
Beckcom, S. M. 41
Beckom, William H. 130

Bennett	68
Benton, Amos	60
Berrien, Hon. John M.	98
Berry, Green	151
Bertin, DR.	74
Bertine	41
Bertine, John M.	41
Big	99, 100
Big Harpe	99, 100
Billups, Henry C., M.D.	133
Birch, Rev. E. P.	147
Bivins, Capt. James M.	54
Blackmon, Mr.	132
Blackshear	80
Blackshear, David and Susan	86
Blacque, Mrs.	73, 74
Blair, Francis P.	126
Blaque, Mrs. Dr.	74
Bliss, Col. John	60
Blossengame, Mr. John	134
Blount, Col. Edmund	55
Blount, Jno.	23
Blount, John S.	22
Blunt	19
Blunt, Master Wm.	31
Boardman, J. M.	56
Boardman, Mr. and Mrs.	57
Bob	148
Bonaparte, Joseph	46
Bonaparte, Lucian	46
Bonaparte, Princess Zenaide Charlotte Julie	46
Bone, Mrs. Elizabeth	83
Bonner, Mr. William Jr.	62
Boon, Mrs. Henrietta	52
Boothe, Mrs. Elizabeth	145
Boothe, Theophilus D.	145
Boyd	81

Boyd, Jack 53
Boyd, John T. 80
Boyle, Mrs. 104
Bozeman, Miss Lizzie 160
Braden's, Dr. Joseph A. 111
Bradford, Dr. 142
Bradley 120
Bradley's, Capt. 120
Brady, John N. 44
Brady, Mr. 45
Brantley, J. W. 118
Brantley, John H. 58, 113
Brantley, Miss Sophronia E. 113
Brantley, Robert. 119
Brantley, W. S. 113
Bray, Mr. William H. 69
Breck, Rev. Bob L. 61
Breck, Rev. R. L. 107, 137
Breckenridge, Mr. 28
Brice, G. 87
Bridges, Miss Sallie R. 11
Bridges, Miss Sarah R. 15
Bridget 87
Brister 93
Brock, Capt. 155
Brooking, Rev. James H. 68
Brooks, Mr. 115, 120
Brooks, Preston S. 126, 138
Brown 127
Brown, Col. George A. 55
Brown, Miss Emily E. 127
Brown, Mr. David P. 99
Brown, Mr. John 54
Brown, Mr. Thos. A. 44
Brown, Mr. Wm. T. 61
Bryan 139
Bryan, Mr. 139

Buchanan, Joseph 99
Bunee, William J. 160
Buntline, Ned 54
Burch, Capt. 70
Burge, Miss Mary Ann E. 116
Burge, Mrs. Amanda 96
Burnett, Martin 73
Burnett, Rev. S. W. 52
Burnett, Rev. Sam'l B. 142
Burnett, Rev. Samuel B. 145
Burr 53
Burr, Aaron 138
Burrell 37
Burroughs, Col. 131
Burroughs, Oliver S. 130
Burrows, Mr. John 87
Burrows, Valentine 87
Burton, Mr. David 77
Butler, Mr. 91
Butler, Prof. 32
Butler, Senator 115, 116

C

C., Mr. 51, 70
C., Mrs. 15
Caldwell, Chan. 94
Caldwell, George W. 155
Caldwell, Hon. P. C. 94
Caldwell, Hon. Patrick Calhoun 94
Caldwell, Mr. 94
Caldwell, Robt. 155
Calhoun, Dr. J. C. 79
Calhoun, John C. 94
Calhoun, Patrick 94
Calloway, Mr. Joel P. 138
Campbell, Brookins 11
Campbell, Mr. 11, 38, 94

Campbell, Mr. John 38
Capers, Bishop 65
Capers, Dr. 65
Capers, Dr. William..65
Carey, Mrs. Martha Ann 34
Carman, Sallie 110
Carney, Mr. John..114
Caroline M., Miss..57
Caroline Matilda, Mrs. 133
Carr, Joseph 27, 74
Carrie V., Miss 113
Carroll, Mr..127
Carruthers, Joseph 27
Carswell, Miss Eugenie 160
Carswell, W. E. 160
Carter, Mr...140
Carter, Mrs. Eliza F. 53
Carter, Walter S...140
Cary...109
Cass, Mrs. 70
Castelaw, Rev. Stephen..32
Castleman, Mr. 51
Cercopely, Mr. George M. 119
Chambles, Miss Rebecca 135
Champion, Dr. Moses 127
Champion, Mrs. E. G. 127
Chaplin, John 89
Chaplin, Mr. 89
Chapman, Eugenius S. 62
Chapman, Mrs. Mary A. E. 58
Chapman, S. T. 44
Chappel, Miss Roixey Ann 144
Chappell, Dr. J. T. 90
Chappell, Mr. William 119
Chappell, T. S. 144
Charles, Prince 46
Charlie 147, 158

Charlie I.	158
Charlotte F., Miss	102
Cheeves, Miss Sarah	145
Childre, Isaac	93
Childre, Miss Martha	73
Childre, Nathan Jr.	73
Childre, Nathan Sr.	73
Chisolm, John	103
Chissom, Thomas Jefferson	101
Chubrick	144
Clanton, Col. N. H.	93
Clapp, Constable	13
Clapp, J. Milton	160
Clark, Miss Ann M.	108
Clay, Cassius M.	79
Clayton, Hon. Thomas	43
Clingman, Thomas	87
Cobb, Col. John A.	95
Cobb, Maj Wm. A.	15
Cobb, Mrs. Jane	15
Cochran, Mr. C. M.	25
Cochrane, Col. Allen	136
Cochrane, T. J.	136
Cocrahn, Jesse	118
Colbert, Jonathan	77
Colbert, Miss Arabella	134
Cole, Mr.	97
Cole, Wm.	97
Collard, Rev. Mr.	68
Collins, Albert	137
Collins, Dr. and Mrs. Robt.	156
Collins, Dr. R.	92
Collins, Mr. Charles and Mrs. Sophia F.	138
Collins, Thomas W.	126
Collins, Thos. W. and Arabella	132
Collins, William	52
Colquitt, Hon. A. H.	72

Colquitt, Hon. Alfred H. 123
Colquitt, Walter T. 72
Colquitte, Mrs. Dolly 72
Colvard, Alpheus 114
Colzy, Dr. E. F. 95, 96
Colzy, Mrs. 96
Colzy, Mrs. Mary Selma 95, 96
Comstock, Deacon 119
Connally, Dr. J. Henry 161
Connelly, Miss Emma V. 133
Conner, Rev. R. A. 109
Connor, Rev. W. G. 61
Conoway, Michael and Jame 71
Cook, Hatch 42
Cook, John R. 119
Cook, Mr. John P. 103
Cook, Rev. Jones E. 55
Cook, Rev. William F. 161
Cope, Thomas P. 58
Cornorell, Dr. 120
Corrigan 88, 89
Cotton, Eliza S. 57
Cowles, Major 156
Cox 109, 151
Cox, Henry H. 154
Cox, Miss Mary V. 11
Cox, Mr. 151
Cox, Rev. Cary 83
Craig, Miss Sallie 68
Cramdock, Paschal D. 127
Crawford, Joseph B. 159
Crawford, Rev. William 54
Crichton, Mr. William 92
Crittenden, Hon. J. J. 32
Crittenden, Mr. 116
Crowder, Mrs. Mary M. 97
Crutchfield, Mr. Thos., Jr. 55

Cullen 12
Cullen, Daniel 12
Culver, Daniel 46
Culverhouse, Hon. G. P. 151
Cumberland, Mrs. Martha and Thomas 93
Cummings, Nathiel 91
Curry 50
Curry, Peter 49, 67
Cuttings, Mr. 28

D

D., Mr. 70
D'Lyon, Col. Isaac 105
Dacy, Mr. John 70
Dalzell, Rev. Mr. 54
Daniels, Jesse 59
Darby, Dolaski Jane 93
Daughtry, Mr. 109
Davis 21, 51, 67, 76, 99, 100
Davis, David D. 51
Davis, Hon. Duncan 158
Davis, Miss Sarah 78
Davis, Mr. 67
Davis, Mr. David J. 67
Davis, Mrs. 27
Davis, Mrs. Paulina W. 26
Davis, Ned 76
Davis, Rev. Dolphin 55
Day 43
Day, Henry C. 42
Day, Hon. Joseph 78, 143
Day, Mrs. Jane 143
Day, R. B. 78
De Bodisco, M. 17
De Waechter, Baron 101
Dean, Col. James 57, 107
Dean, Miss Lizzie S. 107

Dean, Mr. 139
Dean, Mr. James 76
Dean, William A. 61
Deford, Miss 83
Dekay, Capt. James 140
Dekay, Miss 140
Denise 65
Dennis 154
Dettra, Joseph 38
Dick 14
Divine 22, 23
Dixon, Henry 139
Dobbin, Mr. 152
Dockery, Col. John 108
Doctor 110, 135
Dougherty, Mr. 71
Dougherty, Mr. Daniel 71
Downing, Capt. 47
Downing, Captain Samuel W. 47
Drawhorn, Wm. E. M. 80
Driggars, Mr. Daniel S. 108
Driscoll 77
Driskill 101, 102
Drumright, Miss Mary Frances 54
Drysdale, Judge 156
Dudley, Edward B. 92
Dufey, Henry A. 25
Dulin, Rev. Mr. 40
Dumund, E. and Ophelia 154
Duncan, Rev. J. P. 139
Dunlap, Mr. Samuel S. 116
Dunn, Nehemiah and Ann 143
Durham, Mr. Solomon H. 105
Durham, Rev. S. W. 134

E

Earl of Uxbridge 34

Easter	53
Eastham, Miss	105
Edith Mannus	68
Edmunson, Mr.	126
Edwards, James	111
Edwards, Judge	69
Edwards, Rev. Jonathan	69
Eldridge, Mrs. Sarah Payson	99
Eleanor	128
Eliza	57, 84, 157
Eliza A. A., Miss	14
Eliza. Emeline	84
Elizabeth M.	76
Elizabeth, Miss	23, 32, 93
Ella C., Miss	39
Ella Caledocia	75
Ellen A., Miss	99
Ellen C., Mrs.	114
Ellis, Miss Lou	138
Ellis, Wm.	138
Ells, Mr. C. A.	84
Epley	133
Eppeheimer, Wm.	33
Erwin, Elisha	135
Evans	103
Evans, Miss Laura M.	60
Evans, Mr.	142
Evans, Oliver G. & M. A.	152
Evans, Rev. J. E.	151
Evans, Rev. James E.	116, 136
Everett, J. M.	109
Everett, Mr. M.	56
Everlett, Mr.	155
Everlett, P.	155
Evins, James	128
Evins, Rev. J. E.	130

F

Fahrenbaugh. Cephas 101
Fannie Cobb 135
Fannie J. E., Miss 78
Fanny 21, 99, 154
Fant, Dr. 15
Farmer, W. W. 53
Farrar, Dr. George W. 78
Fern Fanny 99
Fidell, John 110
Fields, Mr. 86
Fields, Rev. J. M. 86
Fillmore, Mr. 23
Findley, Rev. David 140
Finney, Dr. Benjamin W. 57
Finney, Mr. John W. 133
Fish, Col. Nicholas 45
Fish, Mrs. 45
Fish, Senator 45
Fitzpatrick, Francis 110
Fitzpatrick, Miss Mary E. 58
Flanders, Capt. David 151
Flint, Mrs. 78
Flournoy, Josiah A. and Anne E. 111
Floyd 139
Floyd, Dr. Adam 139
Flynn, Mrs. 147
Fondee, Mr. Thomas A. 128
Ford 63
Ford, John 22, 23
Forsyth, Miss Josephine B. 122
Fowler 52
Fowler, Bird 52
Fowler, Nathan 121
Frances, Miss 57, 133
Frank 85, 102, 152

Frazer, Mr. 50
Frazer, Mrs. 51
Free, Miss Mary Ann D. 57
Freeman, Miss Benie M. 161
Friedlander, Col. Gustavus 126
Frutrill, Miss Mary J. 134
Fudge, Solomon 15, 111, 157
Fullwood, John Thomas 114
Fulton, C. C. 87

G

G., Mr. 98, 113
Gabriella Augusta 36
Gaillard, Algenon 116
Gamble, Miss Fannie 130
Gamell, Zach 81
Gamusa 44
Gardner, B. R. 112
Gardner, Dr. B. B. 40
Gardner, Lieut. 128
Gardner, Mr. 112, 113
Gardner, Mr. William 61
Garey, Frank P. 102
Garrett, Miss Delilah 139
Garrett, Rev. John 139
Garwood, Mr. Chas B. 122
Gavan, Mr. John 28
Geddings, Dr. Fred 56
George 56, 68, 87, 92, 96, 105, 126, 128, 141, 155, 158
Georgia V., Miss 55, 97
Gibson, Augustus H. 41
Gibson, Mr. Leonard 155
Gibson, Thomas 48
Gilbert, Randolph M. 148
Gilmer, Mr. Edward H. 122
Gilmore, Mr. 52
Giverson, Samuel 110

Glass, Mr. G. P.	98
Glover, Hon. Henry	148
Glover, Nathaniel J.	57
Goddard, Jas.	133
Goddard, Mr.	64
Goddard, William A. B.	64
Godwin, Mr. M. B.	82
Goetz, Andrew	37
Goodloe, David S.	79
Gorham, Joseph	99
Gorham, Miss Susan B.	40
Goss	64
Gould, Jas. G.	48
Gould, Mr.	22
Gowdy, Mr. John	26
Grace, Emily L.	145
Grace, Matthew	146
Grace, Miss Mary Lee	134
Grace, Mr. E. J. M.	134
Grace, Mr. O. T.	139
Grace, Samuel and Nancy M.	146
Graffrey, Peter	54
Grant, Cordelia A.	24
Gray, John D.	87
Gray, Mr. Wm.	87
Gray, Mrs. Anna A.	87
Gray, P. W.	145
Gray, Robert	94
Green	68, 86, 151
Green, Captain Duff	44
Green, Dr. Jas. Mercer	109
Green, George W.	68
Green, Margaret	80
Green, Miss Sarah V.	42
Green, Mr. J. W.	104
Green, Mrs. Emma	104
Green, Squire	103

Greene, Dr. 110
Greer, E. C. 153
Greer, Mrs. Frances M. 153
Gregory, Mr. 19
Griffin 86, 126
Griffin, Alonzo 86
Griffin, David W. 126
Griffin, Larkin 98
Griffin, Miss Geraldine 98
Griffin, Mr. 118
Griffin, Mr. Larkin 35
Grigg 51
Griswold, Samuel 152
Griswold, Wm. H., Junior 133
Groce, Miss Mary L. 62
Guerry James and Margaret 121
Guery, James 102
Gunn 25
Gunn, J. D. 25
Gunn, Miss Brooks 93
Gunter 59, 60
Gunter, Mr. 59

H

H., Mr. 22
H., Mrs. 22, 54
Hadell, Dr. 87
Halee, Mr. William A. 49
Hales, Dr. Wm. 47
Halett 29
Hall, Dr. A. B. 96
Hall, John P. 13
Hall, M. W. 145
Hall, Mrs. Nancy Ann 145
Hamilton 53
Hamilton, Thos. A. 155
Hammond, Dr. 95

Hammond, Miss Antoinette 95
Hammond, Miss Mary C. 54
Hanan, John 70
Hancock, Charles W. 149
Hancock, James 97
Hancock, Mr. 97
Hancock, Rev. G. H. 46, 58, 60
Haralson, Gen. 48
Hardin, Major 122
Hardin, Major E. J. 122
Hardin, Major Edward J. 122
Hardison, Hon. James W. 36
Hardison, Martha 32
Hardison, Mrs. 36
Hardison, Theophilus J. 144
Hare, W. W. 36
Harker, Elizabeth 92
Harney, Dr. J. C. 75
Harpe 99, 100, 101
Harpe, Brothers 99
Harriet 93, 109
Harriet Buel 109
Harris, Col. William G. 14
Harris, Henry 145
Harris, Judge W. 44
Harris, Lieut. 50
Harris, Miss Mary C. 135
Harris, Mrs. 50
Harris, Mrs. Nancy 77
Harris, Rev. Isaac C. 135
Harris, S. W. 143
Harris, Sampson W. 143
Harris, Thomas W. 34
Harry 73
Hart, Mr. James L. 129
Hart, Mrs. 47
Harthon, Mr. William A. 78

Hartly, Mr. Wm. A. 62
Hartwell, Henry 49
Harvey, Albert 96
Harvey, Dr. Richard 75
Harvey, Mr. Henry J. 109
Harvey, Mr. James 22
Harwood, Mrs. 140
Harwood, Rev. E. 140
Haskie 87
Haskie, John 87
Havis, Dr. M. W. 123
Havis, Mrs. Cornelia A. 123
Hay, E. F. 151
Hayden, Mr. Isaac 32
Hays, Jack 22
Hayt 124
Heaving 24
Helen Jane, Miss 119
Henderson 12
Henderson, Rev. Mr. 55
Hendrick, Jacob P. 141
Hendrick, Mr. 141
Henry G. 32
Henry, Mr. Isaac 20
Henry, Samuel 112
Herbert, Hon. P. T. 125
Herndon, Lt. Wm. L. 157
Hibernia R. 88
Hickman, Miss Georgia 97
Hill, Mr. John 85
Hines, John B. 129
Hines, Miss Emma N. 72
Hines, Mr. 129
Hinton, Rev. Mr. 68, 139
Hiser, H. 137
Hodges, J. J. 119
Hodges, J. Joseph and Julia Ann 72

Hodgkins, Miss Martha A. 98
Hoffman, Ogden 115
Holden, Troy G. 142
Holland, Dr. 31
Holland, J. 55
Hollingsworth, J. 154
Hollinsman, John B. 25
Hollis 26
Hollis, Miss Pennie 160
Hollis, Moses 26
Hollis, Mrs. 160
Holmes, Doctor William W. 110
Holmes, Maj. James. 66
Holsey, Mr. Julius H. 134
Holt, Judge Asa 121
Holt, Mr. Patrick H. 56
Holt, Mrs. Irina 56
Holt, Wm. 158
Hopkins, Constable 13
Hortman, Miss Mary 44
Horton, Mr. 53
Hotchkiss 52
Hotchkiss, Buel 52
Hough, Robt. 18
Howard, George T.__ 126
Howard, George Troup 126
Howard, John H. 84
Howard, Major John H. 126
Howard, Mr. 110
Howell 50, 67
Howell Cobb 153
Howland 146
Howland, Thomas 146
Howlett 29
Hoyt, Rev. Dr. 159
Hughes, Archbishop 93
Hughes, Mr. Robert B. 32

Hughes, Wm. L. 32
Hunt 14
Hunt, Archibald 14
Hunter, Capt. John 54
Hurt, Mr. Wm. O. 65
Hutcherson, Richard 144
Hutton, Lieut. 42
Hyller, Elisha 106

I

Irbry, Dr. 16
Irby, Dr. F. W. 15
Itzstein, John Adam Von 89
Ivern, Mr. 13
Ives, Coroner 29
Ives, Miss Emma 117
Ives, Mr. Edwin 117

J

Jackson, Col. J. W. 48
Jackson, Hon. Joseph W. 48
Jackson, Mrs. ?? 47
Jackson, Mrs. Josephine 120
James 11, 18, 31, 42, 47, 48, 66, 69, 71, 72, 75, 78, 90, 97, 98, 102, 109, 110, 111, 118, 121, 122, 128, 134, 144, 147
James Signal 18
Jane M., Miss 147
Jannie, Abraham 110
Jarratt 19
Jarrel, Mr. Levi W. 135
Jarrell, John 57
Jasper 111, 118
Jasper, Rev. T. R. 116
Jennings 159
Jennings, John 159
Jennings, Miss Catherine 67
Jerry 46

Jewett, Charles R. 160
Jewett, Samuel G. 106
Jim 56, 150
Joe 148
John ... 11, 12, 13, 17, 21, 22, 23, 25, 27, 29, 31, 32, 39, 40, 41,
    44, 47, 48, 49, 57, 58, 61, 63, 68, 70, 75, 79, 80, 84, 85, 87,
    89, 92, 94, 101, 103, 104, 110, 113, 114, 119, 123, 128,
    129, 131, 135, 138, 142, 148, 152, 154, 156, 158, 159
John Frederick 123
John G. 29
John Samuel 158
Johne, Col. I.D.N. 54
Johnson 29
Johnson, C. Everette 129
Johnson, Daniel 21
Johnson, Josiah 128
Johnson, Miss C. Helen 61
Johnson, Miss Elizabeth C. 32
Johnson, Miss Rachiel 151
Johnson, Mr. Emmet R. 98
Johnson, Wm. And Louisa 158
Johnston, Mr. Parker E. 97
Johnston, Wm. B. and Anna T. 118
Joiner, Rev. Ebenezer 56
Jones, Donald B. 38
Jones, John 61
Jones, Mr. Abner 89
Jones, Mrs. Mary E. 38
Jordan, Burwell 127
Jordan, Miss Francis M. 60
Judson, Mr. P. M. 57
Judson, P. M. 57
July 149

K

K., Mr. 107, 108, 116, 158
K., Mrs. 130

Kane, Dr. 140
Kane, John...48
Kane, Judge...140
Kansas 35
Keating, Thomas...125
Keit, Hon. L. M. 142
Keith, Rev. W. J. 63
Keitt, Mr. 116
Kelly, James...47
Kelly, Merriland..91
Kelly, Mr. and Mrs...125
Kelly, Mr. P. 134
Kelly, Mr. William M...124
Kelly, Mrs. Julia 134
Kelly, Patrick Henry...134
Kelly, William S. 58, 62
Kelly, Wm. S...154
Kelsey, Mrs. Chloe N. 160
Kelstch, Mrs. Sarah..84
Kelsy, Capt. Noah...160
Kemp, Joseph and Catherine..................................123
Kenan, Mr..158
Kendall, Dr. John B. 109
Kendall, Geo. W. 58
Kennedy, William F. 57
Kent, Miss Mary 122
Kezziah 20
Kikkley, Col. 37
Kilkelly, Capt. 109
Kilpatrick, Mr. William...134
Kilpatrick, Mrs. Francis W. 130
Kilpatrick, William G. 130
Kinder, Frances A. 36
King, Gov. 139
King, James N. and Sarah Ann.................................78
King, James R. and F. P. 109
King, Mr. Henry J...122

King, Mrs. Susan 145
King, William 77
Kirk, Dr. 89
Kirkland 96
Kizziah 40
Knight 158
Knight, George 158
Knight, Wm S. 105
Knowles, Rev. J. 161
Knowles, Rev. Joshua 146
Kornega, Daniel 107
Kornega, Mr. 107

L

Ladd, Mr. 65
Lamar, Miss Evelina G. 122
Lamar, Mr. 14
Lamar, Mr. Zachariah 14
Land, Henry 159
Land, Miss Martha 159
Landermann 74
Landrum, Rev. S. 14, 57, 60, 61, 62, 65, 83, 96, 108, 122, 134, 135, 138
Landrum, Rev. Sylvanus 122, 127, 130, 141
Lane, Col. 143
Lane, Wm. A. 120
Lanier, Master Sidney 31
Laura Ellen, Mrs. 104
Leary C. 155
Leckie, Mr. Thomas 90
Leconte, Miss Anna C. 138
Lee, Miss Josephine Louisa 101
Leonard, James 109
Leonard, Miss Cate 80
Leroy 27
Lester, Mr. James D. Jr. 93
Lester, Rev. Robert 93

Lewis, Lieut. Edward C. 45
Lewis, Mr. Benj. F. 111
Lewis, Mr. William 77
Lewis, Zachariah 107
Lightfoot, Dr. 121
Lilly, Robert M. and Temperance 155
Linch, Lewis 67
Little 99, 101
Little Harpe 101
Little, John 21, 110
Lockett, Mr. B. G. 11
Lockett, Mr. Benjamin 15
Lofley, Miss Ann Elizabeth 111
Lofley, Miss Jane 111
Lofley, Misses 112
Lofley, Mrs. 112
Lofley, Mrs. Margaret 111
Lohman 24
Long, Mrs. 30
Long, Nathaniel 30
Lonry 16
Loring, Charles 41
Lou. J., Miss 161
Lou___, Miss Mary 42
Lounsberry, A. J. 131
Love, Ann Eliza 84
Lowe, Wm H. 95
Loyless, Henry 159
Lucas, Littleberry 128
Lucy B., Mrs. 155
Lucy E., Miss 55

M

M., Mr. 103
M'Lure, Capt. James 90
Macarthy, Francis W. 138
Maddox, Rev. Mr. 54

Madison Abernathy	18
Magrath, Mr. John	104
Malinda, Mrs.	103, 153
Mallary, Rev. C. D.	72
Malsby, Lott	117
Maners, Capt.	140
Maners, Capt. William	140
Mann, Rev. Alfred T.	95
Manora	123
Manuel	136
Marcus	118
Marcy, Mr.	150
Marcy, Wm. L.	150
Margaret	47, 80
Maria Therese	56
Marion, Gen.	21
Marquis of Anglesey	34
Marsh, Charles	48
Marshal, Rev. John	15
Marshall, T. F.	32
Martha Thomas	32
Martin	33, 71, 73, 157
Martin, James	71
Martin, John W.	31, 142
Martin, Miss Fannie	65
Martin, Mr. John G., Jr.	130
Martin, Mrs. E. J.	65
Mary	29, 37, 66, 83, 117, 118, 134, 157
Mary E., Miss	32, 58
Mary Elizabeth	118
Mary Jane	66, 157
Mary Seymour	134
Mary Y., Miss	15
Mask	83
Mason	101, 151
Mason, Mr.	151
Mastick, Jacob	46

Matlack, Esquire...106
Matthews, Justus...98
Mattie..156
Mauldin, Miss Martha C..144
Mausfield, Jos. 68
Mayoress of Washington 35
McAllum, Miss Mary 119
McArthur, Mr. Sam'l 142
McBain...149
McBain, Newman 149
McBride, Mr. 45
McCall, Master Roger..31
McCall, Rev. G. R...119, 159
McCallum, John..27
McCardel 31
McClendon, Mrs. Edith B...29
McCloskey, Mr. 22
McCready, Peter B...138
McDaniel, D...19
McDonald, Hon. C. J..75
McDonald, S. 78
McEackin, J. Wesley..125
McGehee, Dr. Edmund 158
McGlinsey, James...72
McGregor, Mr. Alexander 129
McGuire, Barney...71
McLane, Hon. Louis...157
McMillan, Dr. John...79
McMillan, John R..79
McMillon, Mr. S. J. 11
McNamara, Michael 42
McRea 12
McSwain, Gilbert..46
Meagher, Thomas F...35, 93
Meeks, Mr. J. C. 37
Menard, Col. M. B..129
Menard, Mr. Louis E. 98

Merrell	22
Meschamp, Edward	110
Meyer, Mr.	20
Middlebrooks, Alfred	128
Miller	60
Miller, Andrrew J.	103
Miller, Dr. James Arrington	136
Miller, Matthew, Jr.	110
Millie Pierpont	57
Mills, Green L.	86
Mills, Matilda Ann	110
Mills, Sarah Jane	128
Minor, Col. William	160
Minor, Samuel Wright	160
Mississippi	108
Mitchell, Mrs. J.	69
Mix, Mr.	70
Mix, Mr. William T.	70
Mobley, Alex	85
Montfort, Miss Martha E.	134
Montfort, Mr. Wm. H.	134
Montgomery	148
Moore	146
Moore, Chas.	146
Moore, Mrs. Martha	44
Moore, Wm. M.	49
Moran, John	22, 23
Morgan, Elizabeth	105
Morgan, Jesse	105
Morris, Mr. Boling G.	35
Morris, Mr. Hardy	136
Morris, Mrs. Martha D.	130
Mott, Dr.	73
Mott, Valentine	74
Mowatt, Mrs. Anna Cora	36
Mr. Perkins	154
Mulholland, C. and Adaline S.	88

Munday, Thos. J. 142
Munroe, Mr. 73
Munroe, Nathan C. 73
Mussignano, Prince 46
Myrick, Rev. D. 55

N

Nancy S. 87
Napier, Col. E. Tressillian. 160
Napier, Le Roy 36
Napier, Miss Tabitha E. 67
Nash 60
Nash, Mr. Acton E. 143
Nauman, Col. 114
Nebraska 35
Ned 54, 76
Neel, Miss Sarah A. 142
Nelson, James B. 66
Newland, Mr. 107
Newland, Mr. Jos. 106
Newton, John 135
Nisbet, James T. 134
Nixon, C. W. 157
Nixon, Mr. C. W. 15
Nolan 71
Nora 83
Norman, George 96
Norman, Mrs. 96
Norman, Mrs. Sarah 96
Nowell 50, 67
Nowell, Luke 49, 67

O

O., Mr. J. P. 33
O.,Mr. 38
O'Donohoe, Mr. 17
O'Ferrell, Dr. 35

O'Meally, Martin 33
O'Neil, Rev. Dr. 80
Oatman, Olive 113
Odom, Mr. Orrey 60
Ogletree, Judge David 97
Old Albert 137
Olin, Justice 25
Oliver 35, 130, 139, 152
Oliver Fletcher 152
Oliver, Miss S. E. 55
Oliver, Thomas 139
Oliver, Tom 77
Olmstead, Capt. 44
Olmstead, Capt. Jonathan 44
Orndoff, David 78
Orr, Mr. 60, 79
Orr, Mr. A. J. 79
Osborn 38
Osborne, John H. 75
Osborne, Mrs. 75
Osborne, Mrs. Maria Fossim 75
Oslin, Rev. William W. 97
Ott, Mr. 38
Ouachita 108
Owen, Rev. R. M. 106

P

P., Capt. 62
Pages, Juan 66
Paget, William Henry 34
Palmer, Mr. Walter 103
Parker, Joseph 26
Parker, Stephen W. and Sarah F. 156
Parks 75
Parks, Dr. James J. 141
Parks, James 75
Parton, Mr. James 99

Partridge, Capt. ...16
Partridge, Captain Alden ...16
Paster, Juan ...66
Pat ...36
Patrick, Mr. ...98
Patten ...28
Patten, Mr. James ...28
Patterson ...36
Patterson, Dr. J. C. ...48
Paul, Miss Lucy ...136
Paul, Mr. ...136
Paulk, Mr. Uriah ...97
Peacock ...45
Pearce, Mrs. Lucinda ...130
Pearse, Mr. ...84
Peggy ...104
Pepper, Frank ...152
Perkins, Dr. H. B. ...132
Perkins, Hardy ...154
Perkins, Judge ...132
Perry, D. R. ...98
Perry, Mr. D. R. ...98
Peter ...35, 49, 53, 54, 57, 67, 93, 138, 149, 152
Peter Alonzo ...152
Peters, G. ...105
Pettey, George ...128
Petur, Master Henry ...31
Philbrick, Samuel ...62
Phillips, Mr. James ...145
Pierce, Bishop George F. ...39
Pierce, Mr. ...152
Pierce, Rev. Jas. L. ...146
Pierson, Susan ...43
Pike, Henry ...112
Pintock, J. A. ...116
Pintock, Miss Ophelia D. ...116
Plane, William, F. ...61

Pleasants, Capt. John 46
Poe, Hon. Washington 153
Poe, William 89
Poole 96
Porter, Gen. Peter B. 23
Porter, Miss 23
Porter, Miss Elizabeth 23
Postell, Rev. J. C. 28
Postell, W. F. 158
Poteet, Mr. 133
Pou, Mr. Augustus 131
Powell 113
Powell, O. J. 112
Powers, Hon. A. B. 37
Powers, Hon. Abner P. 126
Powers, Mr. John 37
Pratt's, Capt. 112
Prendergast 22
Prendergast, Captain E. M. 22
Price, Capt. W. B. 42
Prossetter, Captain Ed 43
Proudfoot, Mr. and Mrs. 76
Pryor, Mr. 126
Purifoy, Dr. Adolphus 52
Putnam 28
Putnam, Wm. B. 28

Q

Quin, John 23, 85
Quinn 71
Quinn, Mr. John 85

R

Rabun, Gov. 86
Ragland, John B. 29
Railroad 108
Raines, Mary S. 29

Rainey, Mr. 18
Rainey, Signal 18
Raley 67
Ralston 14
Ralston, Wm. A. 14
Ramsey, Joseph B. 35
Rand 13
Rand, John 12
Ratliffe, Miss Eliza 133
Rawls, John 142
Ray, Dr. Duncan W. 54
Rayley, Gen. T. H. 120
Rebecca 114, 118
Rebecca Ann 118
Rebecca J., Mrs. 114
Red River 108
Redding, H. F. 36
Redding, Mr. 37
Rees, Rev. H. R. 98
Reese, Rev. Mr. 67
Renfro, Miss Augusta Ann 55
Renfroe, James T. 78
Renfroe, Jas. T. 135
Restell, Madame 24
Revell, Henry Y. 73
Reynolds 82, 127
Reynolds, Charles P. 83
Reynolds, Miss Mary J. 30
Reynolds, Mr. L. O. 82
Reynolds, William 57
Rhind, James 48
Rhodes, Miss Mary A. E. 83
Rhodes, Robert 105
Rice 77, 101, 102
Richards, Alex. 161
Richards, Wm. C. and Caroline H. B. 68
Richardson, Miss Fannie E. 60

Ricker, Mr.	17
Ricker, Mr. Edward F.	17
Ridgely, F. L.	73
Ridgway, Mr.	126
Riley, David F.	104
Riley, Jacob.	123
Riley, Mr. John J.	142
Ritchie, Miss Amanda R.	105
Ritchie, Wm. F.	36
Robert Atkinson	92
Roberts, Dr.	11
Roberts, Miss Rebecca R.	126
Roberts, Miss Sallie E.	146
Roberts, Mr. A.	74
Roberts, Mrs. Helen M.	74
Robertson, John M.	104
Robertson, Nathan C.	104
Robinson, A. M.	81
Robinson, Alexander M.	80
Rodgers, Mrs. H.	54
Roff, A.A.	17
Root, Ezra	144
Roquemon, Rev. Jas.	35
Rose, John.	101
Rose, Wm.	72
Ross, J. B.	113
Ross, Jesse W.	61
Ross, Jno. B.	83
Ross, Master Frank	31
Ross, Miss Victoria	31
Ross, Rev. Dr.	107
Row, Mr. Daniel	106
Rowe, Miss	109
Ruddel	90
Ruddel, Joseph	90
Rufus	80
Rush, Miss Caroline	46

Rush, Mrs. 158
Rusk, Gen. 153
Russell, Waring 22
Rutherford, E. 36

S

S. Landrum, Rev. 14, 57, 60, 61, 62, 65, 83, 96, 108, 122, 134, 135, 138
S., Judge 30
S., Mrs. 91, 139
Sadifur, Henry 44
Sage, Mrs. Mary 65
Sallie 86, 110
Sam 117
Samuel, Reuben 35, 93
Samuels, Reuben 35
Sanders, Elizabeth 107
Sanders, Miss Rhoda 58
Sanders, Mrs. 58
Sara Lawton 111
Sarah A., Mrs. 129
Sarah Sophia 138
Sartorius 43
Saul 29
Saunders, Professor J. Milton 39
Sayers, George W. 56
Scales, Mr. Robert W. 65
Schlissinger, Col. 117
Schlumgen, Mr. Freidchrich 61
Scholey, Mrs. Catherine 78
Scott, E. W. 147
Scott, Miss Ellendra F. 58
Scott, Mr. 147
Scovill 67
Scovill, Samuel 67
Seag, Thomas 35
Shackford 24

Shackford, Geo. R. 24
Shade, Mrs. 110
Shangle, Officer 72
Sharp, M. R. 19
Shaw, Harvey W. and William 149
Shaw, Mr. William H. 135
Shaw, William 149
Shaw, Wm. 149
Sheldon, Mr. 135
Shephard, William B. 42
Shepherd, Hon. D. C. 134
Sherman, John 40
Sherry, Miss Elphany 60
Shine, Mr. 122
Shive, Mr. 136
Shive, Mr. and Mrs. 136
Shivers, Col. Wm. Jr. 86
Shivers, Mrs. Susan F. 86
Shockley, Mr. John R. 67
Short 45
Shorter, Col Eli S. 41
Sikes, J. F. and N. 147
Simmons 139
Simmons, John and Martha 156
Simmons, Thos. J. 160
Simon, Pantleon 47
Sims, Miss Mary B. 69
Singleton, Dr. 30
Singleton, Dr. Joseph J. 30
Sintapower, Margaret 47
Slatter, Mrs. Nancy 109
slave 19, 38, 87, 93, 117, 152
Sledge, Isham D. 127
Slocumb, Stephen 37
Smiley, R. B. 80
Smith 11, 13, 72
Smith, Clay 79

Smith, Dr. J. Dickson ... 113
Smith, George A. ... 141
Smith, James Y. ... 110
Smith, John ... 11
Smith, Matilda C. ... 105
Smith, Miss ... 83
Smith, Mr. ... 59
Smith, Mr. Asa ... 46
Smith, Mr. David M. ... 134
Smith, Mr. Hardy ... 13
Smith, Mrs. Elizabeth G. ... 24
Smith, Mrs. Gen. ... 121
Smith, Rev. Blakely ... 122
Smith, Rev. D. L. and Mrs. Amanda N. ... 116
Smith, Rev. Davis ... 160
Smith, Rev. Joesph T. ... 55
Smith, Rev. O. L. ... 97
Smith, Rev. Wesley ... 134
Smith, Silas ... 72
Smith, Stephen S. ... 110
Smith, Thomas G. ... 105
Snow, Miss Helen A. ... 151
Sol ... 149
Solomon, Col. Henry ... 130
Solomon, Henry F. ... 58
Solomon, Lewis and Lucy Ann F. ... 49
Solomon, Miss Geraldine C. ... 130
Solomon, P. ... 98
Solomon, Peter ... 35
Solomon, Rev. L. ... 58, 83
Solomon, Rev. Lewis ... 90, 130, 142, 154, 159
Sontag ... 36
Sontag, Henriette ... 36
Sorrel, Thomas ... 117
Southard, Reuben ... 93
Southerlin, Reuben ... 35
Spear, Dr. ... 154

Spear, Rev. Eustace 54
Speer, Alex. M. and Mary A. 116
Speer, Dr. 154, 155
Speer, Rev. A. 154
Speir, Mr. William C. 92
Speir, Rev. E. W. 113
Spence, Charles 41
Spence, William 41
Spencer, Robert 48
Spier, Mr. Washington 36
Spivey, Mr. 132
Spivey, Mr. Eli 132
Stanley, Ira 90
Stanley, Miss H. A. 90
Steele, Capt. George 107
Steele, Miss Ellen E. 107
Stembridge, John 154
Stephen 32, 37, 54, 110, 156, 157
Stephens, Miss Sarah Ann 32
Stewart, Miss P. Mary J. 141
Stiff, Edward Sr. 32
Stiles, Benj. E. 71
Stiles, Benjamin E. 70
Stock 102
Stocking 101, 102
Stoddard, David 79
Stone, Mr. Jesse 148
Story, R. J. 109
Stoughton, Sergeant 72
Strang 122
Strang, James J. 122
Strickland, Mr. G. W. 130
Stubbs, Mr. 90
Stubbs, Mr. Seaborn J. 90
Stubbs, Mrs. 90
Stubbs, Mrs. Salina 90
Sturgis, Hon. Jos. 30

Sturgis, Judge 30
Stuyvesant, Governor 45
Sumner 115, 120
Sumner, Mr. 115
Sumner, Senator 115
Susan Mary 118
Sweeney, Mark 63
Swift, Col. George P. 106

T

T., Mr. 159
Tabor, John...68
Taggart, Mrs. Malinda 103
Talek, J. O. 88
Talfound, Thomas Noon 29
Taliaferro, Miss Anne W. 147
Talmage, Rev. Dr. S. K. 134
Tarver, Gen. H. H. 72
Taylor, Charles...17
Taylor, Cornelia J. 17
Taylor, Miss Laura J. 130
Taylor, Miss Margaret A. 106
Taylor, Mr. Joe E. 63
Taylor, Mr. Joshua...111
Taylor, William 113
Tell, Wm. 33
Tharp, Mr. 67
Tharp, Mrs. Elizabeth 152
Thigpen, Rev. A. M. 99
Thigpen, Rev. Alex M. 133
Thigpen, Rev. Alex. P. 135, 147
Thomas29, 34, 35, 36, 46, 48, 52, 58, 78, 87, 93, 98, 101, 105, 114, 117, 125, 126, 132, 139, 146, 156
Thomas Clarence 78
Thomas D...36
Thomas G..46, 105
Thomas W..34, 58, 126, 132

Thomas, C. R. 147
Thomas, Dave 52
Thomas, Mr. 90, 111, 121, 128
Thomas, Mrs. Martha 110
Thompson, Dr. Charles S. 37
Thompson, Dr. Chas. S. 37
Thompson, Miss Mary 37
Thompson, Peter 53
Throop, Col. 12
Throop, Col. O. H. 12
Tissereau, Mr. T. 96
Todd, Mr. Sr. 32
Tolliard, Andrew 28
Tom 64, 77
Towle, Frederick 159
Townsend, Miss 93
Townsend, Peter 93
Townsend, Walter B. 17
tracheotomy 96
Tracy, E. 31
Tracy, Edward D. 107
Tracy, P. 142
Trapp, Miss Lucia M. 61
Travis, Wm. 33
Troup, Ex-Governor 114
Troupe, Gov. 50
Troutman, Mr. H. A. 67
Trump 94
Trump, G. A. 94
Trump, Mrs. Margaret 94
Tucker, Mr. John W. 15
Tucker, Sterling 32, 46, 135
Turnbull, Col. Walter 28
Turner, Mr. John 39
Tyner, K. 116
Tyner, Mrs. 116
Tyner, Mrs. Martha 116

U

Union 27

V

Van Buren, Ex-President 132
Van Buren, Mr. 132
Vandyke, Dr. 133
Vasage, James 98
Virginia W., Miss 109
Visage, Samuel W. 128
Visage, Wm. H. 105

W

Wagnon, Miss Margaret A. 135
Wait, John 47
Wait, Mr. 47
Waldin, Peyton 31
Wales, Mr. Asaph 94
Walker, C. H. 57, 73, 77, 98, 105, 107, 128
Walker, C.H., J.P. 57, 73, 98, 107
Walker, Caleb 18
Walker, Caroline M. 142
Walker, Eli 123
Walker, George W. 87
Walker, Mr. 123
Walker, Mr. S. W. 60
Wallan, Fannie W. 47
Walsm, Mike 82
Walter R. 116
Walter, Dr. 39
Walters, Mr. 78
Wampole, Mr. 38
Ward, G. F. 40
Ward, Mat. 32
Warren, Rev. J. L. 133
Washington, James H. R. and Mrs. Mary Ann 118

Washington, John Marshall 17
Watkins, Marshal 69
Watts, Mr. Wm. B. 143
Webster 89
Webster, Daniel 34
Weed, Edwin B. 11
Weed, Henry W. 115
Weed, Mr. E.B. 11
Weed, Mrs. E. B. 115
Weeden, Mr. William H. 55
Weems, Rev. J. J. 85
Welborn, Oliver 35
Wells 11
Welsh, Patrick 95
West 151
West, Luke 35
West, William 148
Westbrook, Mr. John 68
Weymouth, Capt. Bourdette 109
Whitaker, Miss Eleanor Elizabeth 73
White 78
White, Miss Laura A. E. 109
White, Wm. 33
Whitesides 159
Whittington, Mr. E. O. 60
Whittle, Mr. 118
Wilcox, Miss Martha 85
Wilcox, Woodson 85
Wilder, Mr. Benjamin F. 136
Wiley, Miss Mary C. 137
Willett, Miss Martha M. 83
William .34, 41, 42, 49, 52, 57, 58, 61, 62, 64, 77, 80, 89, 113,
    121, 130, 137, 148, 149, 160
Williams 46, 96, 123
Williams, Alexander 33
Williams, Col. William 154
Williams, Francis 95

Williams, John L. ... 128
Williams, Joseph ... 95
Williams, Miss Mary Virginia ... 154
Williams, Mr. G. Jackson ... 60
Williams, Sarah Caroline ... 98
Williams, Thomas Nelson ... 98
Williamson, Miss Victoria E. ... 145
Williford, Joel ... 30
Wilson ... 13, 32, 59
Wilson, J. V. ... 112
Wilson, John ... 32
Wilson, Joseph ... 13
Wilson, Miss Malinda ... 86
Wilson, Prof. ... 32
Wilson, Samuel ... 59
Winchester, Mr. ... 92
Wingfield, Junius ... 134
Winn, Dr. David R. E. ... 57
Winn, Miss Julia C. ... 63
Winn, Mr. Jonathan D. ... 127
Winship, Emory ... 157
Winship, Isaac ... 104
Winters, Mr. ... 101
Wise, John ... 92
Wise, Wm. ... 69
Wittich, L. L. ... 27
Wittich, President ... 27
Wood ... 22, 40, 146
Wood and Tomlinson ... 40
Wood, Irwin J. ... 58
Woodard, Stephen ... 32
Woods, Mr. Warren D. ... 69
Woods, Rev. Leonard ... 43
Woodson, Dr. Creed Taylor ... 140
Woodward, Mr. A. L. ... 95
Woolf, Miss Statira ... 128
Wooton, Miss Nancy C. ... 129

Wooton, Rev. John 129
Wright 53, 54, 82
Wright, Arminius 42
Wright, David 80, 81
Wright, Mr. Robt. E. 32
Wright, Rev. Arminius 97